I FEEL...

I FEEL...

Emotions – For Teens, By Teens

Parker Jones

Cover designed by Parker Jones

Parker Jones
Visit my website at
https://withParker.com

Printed in the United States of America

First Printing: May 2019
Jones NW Creative
https://jonesnw.com

ISBN-9781097107964

This book is dedicated all teens, for all our mental and emotional challenges throughout our teenage years.

A portion of any profits generated by this book will be donated to support teen mental health programs.

But feelings can't be ignored, no matter how unjust or ungrateful they seem.

— ANNE FRANK, THE DIARY OF A YOUNG GIRL

CONTENTS

ACKNOWLEDGMENTS

Many people supported my goal of writing and publishing this book, and I want to thank each of them for their contribution.

I want to thank Mackenzie Morris for contributing to the chapter on Anxiety. I also want to thank the contributors for the chapters on Bullying & Social Anxiety, though they wish to remain anonymous.

For contributing by brainstorming the initial list of feelings – as well as ideas and suggestions – thank you to my classmates and friends. I couldn't have done it without you.

Thanks to Stephanie Carbajal and Emily Dickinson for editing and thanks to Dyame Lemming, JoAnna Dickinson and Marisol Gutierrez for review and constructive feedback.

Finally, I want to thank my Dad for encouraging me to write during the National November Month of Writing (http://nanowrimo.org/), and never wavering in his support through each step from start to publication.

FORWARD

This is an inspiring book for youth, written by a youth on different negative emotions that they may feel.

In writing about those emotions, Parker provides his own perspectives and experiences to engage and connect with teen readers, encouraging them to try hard, do well, embrace their uniqueness and work to understand others.

Ultimately, this book lets readers know that they are not alone in confronting the challenges presented by emotions during their teenage years.

This book is not clinical, but includes a section identifying available resources for those that may be experiencing emotions that are impacting day to day life. If you or someone in your life is struggling in this way, please don't hesitate to use those resources.

JoAnna Dickinson, MSW

INTRODUCTION

This book was born from a joke to myself that I needed a book of advice because I seemed to be having the same conversations again and again with my friends. Once I said it out loud and thought about it, I soon realized that I'm not the only one who needs this book-we all do.

The coolest part about the book is that I also asked my friends to share their feelings and emotions with which they struggle. I never heard the same emotion more than once or twice, which shows the spectrum of what teens experience.

We all go through hardships and struggles. This book is written by teens for teens, for we all need a little encouragement in this world.

Now, I don't know where you are in your life, what issues you've face, or who you are. Some of you might have someone in your life who knows what you've been through, or maybe no one does, or perhaps you picked up this book today because you want something to help you through this crazy world.

The best advice I can give you is to keep an open mind while you read through these pages. I hope you'll find some words of inspiration in this book. I also encourage you to find someone you trust and talk to them. I hope that for every feeling of negativity, you will also find a positive perspective.

Allow your opinions to be changed. You can choose. Seek advice, find perspectives, discuss, reflect, improvise, and overcome.

You are worthy, and I believe in you. I wish to be part of your process and contribute to your discussions, your seeking and hopefully, let you know that no matter what you feel, others like my friends and me are right there with you.

ABANDONED

*Man's greatest actions are performed in
minor struggles. Life, misfortune, isolation,
abandonment and poverty are battlefields
which have their heroes - obscure heroes who
are at times greater than illustrious heroes.*
—Victor Hugo

U nfortunately, nothing in this world is permanent. Things and people come
and go. Even those we care about very dearly.
Heartbreak, loss, and betrayal are just a few things that can leave us
feeling abandoned. We can be abandoned by the ones we love and trust, by life,
even by the person we wish we were.

We may have other friends, but this emotion leaves us feeling alone. It creates
a sense of loss and a hole in our heart. We can only feel lost if we were first found.
Many feelings may come from abandonment but remember that if someone leaves,
it isn't your fault. It is their choice and action, and that doesn't take away from
how great you are.

The interesting thing is, at some point in your life, you will leave someone
behind as well. When things and people drift away, we feel alone. We hide our pain
on the inside. We may even build a wall, because the more we let someone in, the
more painful it is if they walk away.

Separation, whether physical or mental, can change us. We try to protect
ourselves, so we don't feel abandoned again. In the time of hardship, it seems
reasonable, it seems okay, to push everyone away. Is it though? Or, maybe you are
just leaving first? You can't stop people from leaving. That is life. You also can't
keep them from leaving by never letting them get close. Saving yourself from a

bad relationship at the expense of a potentially great relationship robs you of experiencing good and great moments together.

Traumatic experiences scare us, and fear changes us. I have felt abandoned. I too was scared. I hid all the negative emotions inside.

I felt as if no one would care, and that no one understood. I blamed myself, yet I knew I couldn't live like that. I was scared, but I also had nothing to lose. I let one person in and told them my problems. Through this person, I learned to trust and love.

It's easy to hold on to your bad memories and past painful experiences. You can't prevent breakups or people moving on, and it's okay to feel alone and lonely. Yes, it hurts, but a time comes when you will move on too.

I think relationships and connections can be a big part of the solution. All it takes is one good connection. Find a friend, build trust, and let them into your life and your secrets. This is a step towards healing.

Everything happens for a reason. Both good and bad times lead to current and future times. Life is growth. Someone may leave. Try to learn from the experience instead of letting it hold you back or choosing to hate.

Learn to love yourself, for you will always have you. If someone leaves you in a time of need, they may not be the friend you deserve. Invest yourself into the friends who stay in your life, value them, and this can help fight your feelings of abandonment.

It's natural to want to blame, to be angry or sad over a loss from your life. When someone leaves, for whatever reason, that is on them. They may feel the loss too, or it may be they had no choice or even made the best choice for themselves at the time.

Go out there and live life and try to put the past behind you. Find a healthy coping method. Make connections and seek new friends. You can do amazing things, don't let one moment in time ruin the rest.

AFRAID

*Don't be afraid of your fears. They're not there
to scare you. They're there to let you know
that something is worth it.*
—C. JoyBell C

Afraid, the feeling of fear. Fear is worrying about an outcome and anticipating it before it resolves. The problem with fear is that it's hard to beat-it is also hard to even understand why you are afraid sometimes.

While healthy fear has its place in life, fear also limits us. It stops us from fixing problems, from being productive, from doing good and changing the world.

What we're afraid of is different for every single person in every different situation. Our natural fearful feelings will try to stop us. This emotion even goes as deep as being afraid to admit our fears. Fear could have even stopped me from writing this.

I didn't let my fears win though and neither should you.

Think back to a time where you were afraid, and you let fear keep you from doing something. Now think about it, what do you feel? Regret? Shame? Relief?

If you had done the thing that fear prevented you from doing, maybe your fears *would* have come true. That's the thing - you do not know, and you may never know. That's why fear is such a difficult emotion.

We all fear things-and the range of human fears ranges from the common, such as fear of death, to the seemingly insignificant for a majority of people. For example, *geniophobia*, the fear of chins, or *genuphobia*, the fear of knees or kneeling.

There's nothing wrong with these fears, but just like any other fear, they place limits. Your fears can stop you, if you let them. It may feel perfectly normal to let fear stand in our way, but *normal* does not always correlate to a good outcome.

The good and bad news is that confronting fear, and trying to overcome it, is an opportunity we will each get many times in our life.

Think of your fear as a person. The person is trying to be helpful, but their only method is to stop you from doing something. Should you let this one person stop you from doing something for absolutely no reason? I hope not, because we can choose to be better and stronger than our fears.

If you have a fear of heights, one of way to overcome it is going up a little bit higher each day. Overcome the smaller fear, before approaching the larger one. Is it really a fear of heights or of falling? Very few people fall from heights, so what do we even fear? But when we refuse to go somewhere, we keep ourselves from an experience.

You are the only one to decide whether your fear is one you should overcome. Don't do anything that would cause yourself harm. If your scared of fighting a shark, well that is a fear that may save you.

Try to overcome your irrational fears, because fear is just a reaction. You may not be able to stop that reaction, but you can decide not to let it control you.

Fear is tough. There is no guarantee you can overcome your fears, but you can try. In fact, that is all you can do. Try. No one deserves to be stopped from reaching their potential, making a good memory, or finding a good opportunity because of fear. Remember that fear limits us, but it doesn't have to define us.

Put yourself out there. Life is too short for regret. You don't want to live the last hours of your week, month, year, or life looking back and talking about what you should have done. You should look back and see all the things you can say you're glad you did.

AGGRIEVED

When you are aggrieved you learn.
—James Cook

No doubt, there is mistreatment of others all the time. People can be straight-up jerks-and other words I probably shouldn't say. There is usually a reason people act like this-fear, humiliation, embarrassment, a bad example in their life-but it doesn't make their actions right. Unfair treatment still hurts. Sometimes it makes us feel like we may deserve it.

You never deserve it. You deserve positivity. So, find positive people and things and hold onto them.

When you hear the word "rude," does a friend come to mind? Someone else? Negative people are often rude. They are mean to you and treat you poorly. Maybe many people come to mind. Life in general may be rude to you. Always kicking at your heels.

One thing people are really good at is letting things like this slide by. Don't. Sometimes life will hurt you, and there is nothing you can do about it. Other times, you need to stand up for yourself. If there is negativity with a friend, talk with them. If it still doesn't stop, you can't stand for that. Don't let someone aggrieve you.

This can also be situational, one way to stand up for yourself is to get help. Bullying, for example, may require you to find an adult you trust but it also your duty to stand up and find that help.

People are rude for their own reasons. Do what you can to stop this negativity; it doesn't help them or you. Be honest with your friends and family, and speak up against it. You don't deserve to be mistreated, so if you are, do something about it.

Advocate for yourself, because no one else will. Surround yourself with positive people. Good people are out there, everywhere-seek them out. Hold them close and let them know their worth.

You know what it's like to be mistreated, so treat others well. Shower them with kindness, even the ones who don't do the same in return. You don't have to be friends with everyone, but be nice. Negativity is everywhere. If you can't change the way a person treats you, dissolve the connection with them. It would be contradicting to remove negative people from your life but be negative yourself.

Surround yourself with people who treat you better than you deserve to be treated. When life aggrieves you, remember that there are good times and bad. If you give up in the bad times, you don't live for the good times, and all of your life will feel bad. Stay strong and advocate for yourself. Nothing great comes easy.

AGITATED

*I feel agitated all the time, like a hamster in
search of a wheel.*
—Carrie Fisher

Agitation, a feeling of annoyance, uneasiness, or even anger, is caused by things that really grind our gears. The interesting thing about agitation is that the more agitated we are, the easier it is to get agitated over little things.

A lot of things can agitate us, both reasonable and not. Reasonable things that may agitate us are acts of injustice in society. Unreasonable things might be physical characteristics of a person, unchangeable things, or biased opinions.   .

Being agitated can cause us to lash out, so it's important to learn to keep our cool. One of the best ways to do this is stepping out and looking at what is agitating you from a new perspective.

An assortment of things will agitate you-it isn't preventable. One thing that can be controllable is how you react. Situations and other people cannot be controlled, not easily at least. Don't spend your energy on trying to control the things that cannot be controlled, with fixing unfixable circumstances. You will burn out and likely be more agitated with the lack of results.

Instead, control the controllable. Hate may build up inside, but deal with it by venting or talking to someone. This way your hateful speech isn't spurted out in anger and agitation. The world's biggest evils derive from hate not taken care of appropriately.

Agitation is normal and common. Many things can make you agitated-- sometimes it just happens because you're grumpy or in a bad mood. Although it is not easy, try to remain peaceful.

It's easy to let agitation take over who you are or control you, but you won't gain much from this. The strongest-willed people can control their anger.

There are right and wrong times to express the way you feel. There are also right and wrong ways to express anger. Know the difference, and express your anger in the right way at the right time. This will bring you more success in changing something than an outburst of hate. Hate only adds to the fire.

Unfortunately, some people will try to rile you. They want to agitate you and make you angry to get a reaction. The best defense is to remain calm. Of course, it's okay to be mad, to feel hatred sometimes. But deal with it smartly.

Stay true to who you are, and don't let your emotions become who you are. Feelings of hate and anger aren't always controllable, but the way you express those emotions is. Trust your mind in time of agitation, not your gut. Keep your cool, and control the controllable.

ANGRY

For every minute you remain angry, you give
up sixty seconds of peace of mind.
—Ralph Waldo Emerson

A nger is an emotion that can be hard to describe. When we don't like the way things are going, maybe in life or maybe in just one moment, a feeling of steam builds up inside. Like a volcano, we could erupt at any moment, or spew little bits of lava at different times. It depends on the situation and the person.

We can feel anger subtly, harshly, or even violently. What happens to make us angry is 99 percent of the time caused by things that we cannot change or influence. How we react to the situation, however, is 100 percent controlled by us.

You shouldn't feel like a bad person because you're angry. When we are angry, we know. Subtle anger means we are little more than annoyed, but may not go out of our way to lash out.

Harsh anger is often the result of a long string of circumstances not going our way; you might also feel harsh anger when you struggle to keep your cool in one specific scenario.

Violent anger can be caused by holding harsh anger inside, or experiencing something so unfavorable that we can no longer control ourselves and our temper.

All three types of anger can be confusing; you usually know when you are angry, but you may not always know why. When those angry feelings set in, try to identify which type of anger it is. Depending on the anger type, there are different methods of dealing with this emotion.

You know yourself better than I do, and you may have a punching pillow or other anti-anger systems in place. That's great! But many of us feel angry and trapped, like we are ready to explode. If you do nothing with your feelings, you may, in fact, explode, so help yourself.

Subtle anger is challenging, but if something is bothering or annoying you, try to take a calm, cool approach. Address and assess the situation, and do your best to solve your problems if you can. Often, we cannot control everything, so be patient. It's not always easy, but fight the temptation to give in.

Harsh anger sucks. When we experience this emotion, we may be what people call "pissed," and that's an accurate description. Often, you want to do something about a situation but don't because you know it isn't the best option.

You may also feel anger building up from different parts of life, and they just stack up and do not stop. Ranting and talking about how you are feeling with someone is a good outlet.

You deserve to be heard, you are not stupid, and keeping everything inside is a terrible idea. Take it from someone who did and lost himself. Find a way to express anger healthily before it gets out of hand.

Violent anger is the out-of-hand scenario, when you feel nothing is going your way, when all you want is for someone to feel your pain and anger.

You feel the need to punch a hole in the wall, because it seems rational. The absolute desire to destroy something overcomes you. If you let this kind of anger sit, it will boil and it will rot who you are and make you do things you may regret.

Find someone you trust and talk to them. Punch a pillow or get a punching bag. Find yourself outside of the anger, and do everything you can to stay true to yourself. You need to release this anger and find coping methods that work for you, rather than hide it. Locking anger inside doesn't make it go away, so deal with it, specifically if it is hard. Not feeling the anger yourself? Be there for someone else who needs to let go and rant.

Anger is the cause of so much destruction in the world. Imagine the security in getting rid of this anger safely. Don't feel wrong or uncared for. You are loved. Whatever is making you angry, I'm sorry. There was a time when anger consumed not only who I was, but what I did. I would hate to see this happen to anyone else.

Take control of your emotion and be who you are. Never let anger or circumstances or people change you for the worse.

ANNOYED

People, circumstances, and situations can all cause a type of anger and lack of patience known as annoyance. Being annoyed is ... quite annoying. Annoyance is a feeling that we all know. You just want something to stop, really, and when it doesn't stop, it can cause us to feel slightly angry--annoyed. Tension builds up as well.

Annoyance is very diverse. Depending on what annoys you and how annoyed you are, you may find different solutions. Think of annoyance as little sparks inside you; you just have to make sure those sparks don't start a fire.

When we hear the word "annoyed" or "annoying," we probably think of a person, me included. This person is just not the type that matches your personality, and you may not like them. This is normal.

But life is a lot of how you look at it, and you'll be surprised by how un-annoying someone is if you first decide to give them patience. It's good to do the following two things.

First, begin to wonder why you may think someone is annoying. They might be the way they are because of something in their past, or something ongoing in their life. People are great at empathy, so have some. You may be holding a grudge against a certain type of person without even realizing it. Let go of that and give people a chance. Like you, everybody is just trying to fit in.

Second, have patience. When you are annoyed, that anger starts to boil, and if you let it steam to a certain point, you'll probably do something you will regret. Exercise your virtues-patience and love. Annoying people will always be around. Find that place in your heart that doesn't let others annoy you.

People aren't the only thing that can annoy us; circumstances and events can annoy us too, mostly situations that can be challenging to get out of or overcome.

Life in general can be annoying, because it keeps throwing little obstacles in our way. We can feel completely overtaken and done. When annoyed, it's easy to give up, or give half your effort. So, try to find peace and a reason why you are in the situation. Think of the lessons you are learning, the self-improvement, the progression. All these things are stronger than temporary annoyance. Giving up or giving in are temptations to overcome. We must realize that life gets annoying sometimes, and accept it. When it is time to refocus, do it.

The annoyances of life and people try to curb us. They are obstacles, but like any obstacles, they can be overcome. Never let the feelings of hate and anger that annoyance bring control you. It's okay to be annoyed and to express it in a reasonable, manageable way. It is less than ideal to be annoyed and let that affect your choices.

It's good to be annoyed by things that need to be changed, and perhaps the sparks could light a fire of change. Mostly, annoyance creates a lot of negativity. There are positive emotions out there that are stronger than annoyance. Find them, use them, and become them.

ANXIOUS

Nothing in the affairs of men is worthy of
great anxiety.
— Plato

T his chapter is written by a good friend of mine. I have tried to learn what
anxiety truly is, but I didn't think I could do it justice. If you have ever felt
true, harsh anxiety, consider getting help. Below is a passage written by
someone who experiences severe anxiety.

You are not alone; there are millions in the world suffering from anxiety. Talk
to a trusted friend or family member, and if you think you might need help, ask
for it. Your life is more important than any material object in this universe. Every
life is equally valuable. I hope these words inspire you to fight the fight. If you are
looking for a less serious chapter, see Stressed.

Anxiety. The feeling of worry, doubt, fatigue, panic, and more. The list goes on
and on. Some people deal with more challenging anxieties than others, but
everyone has them.

Some anxieties feel small, and some feel big, but they're always there following
you. Sometimes, no matter how hard you try to stop those anxieties, you can't.

Stress and feeling overwhelmed can both trigger anxiety. Anxiety comes in
many shapes and forms at any given moment. Having trouble with friends or your

significant other, taking a test, the death of a loved one. These situations can all cause anxiety.

For some people, just the thought of leaving the house or having to see someone can freak you out. Ask yourself this: do you ever catch yourself making plans but never going through with them because you overthink every situation that could happen? This might be anxiety. It sucks, but there are many ways you can overcome it and gain confidence.

If your anxiety relates to another person, talk to them prior and explain why you are nervous, so you are on the same page, and hopefully your fears slowly disappear. You can overcome it step by step. It will take time, and that's okay.

You may be wondering what other things you can do to help yourself overcome anxiety. Because anxiety is different for each person, these suggestions may or may not help, but they are worth trying.

Trying new things may be scary, but it can help easy anxiety.

Sleeping. Sleep heals you; that's what my mom always told me when I was sick. I live by it.

Talking to a trusted adult, close friend, or a mental health hotline. This helps more than anything else. Having supportive friends and family will make you feel safe and accepted, even when you are struggling. Knowing that someone cares and is there for you makes a huge difference.

Writing, reading, listening to music, or drawing may help. Get off your phone or away from the TV and focus on yourself and your creative side. This will make you not think about the negativity of life.

Finding a passion and focusing on that, instead of destructive thoughts.

Going on a run or walk. Put in headphones and jam out to your favorite song. Exercise is great to get things off your mind. When exercising, you only think about how much pain you're in (from the exercise) or how much farther or longer you have to go. You don't think about anything else. Exercise is an escape from reality, which I know we all need sometimes. Try to find what makes you happy.

In the end, anxiety doesn't just go away. You have to fight hard, harder than you may have ever before. Don't let anxiety overtake your life. You are not defined by your anxieties. You are strong, worthy, important, and amazing in every way. Never be ashamed of who you are. You are more than the mistakes you've made. Take care.

I have seen anxiety from the outside and if you too see a friend or loved one struggling with serious anxiety, be there for them. Try to understand the issue; we all have our own struggles. Do not be part of the problem, and learn what helps and what doesn't help. Everyone deals with anxiety differently, so be personal, but above all, be there.

ASHAMED

*Dogs have boundless enthusiasm but no sense
of shame. I should have a dog as a life coach.*
— *Moby*

Here is something we all know but easily seem to forget-no one is perfect, and everyone messes up. Knowing this, and what you may have done, it may feel right to be ashamed.

Shame is something we feel as a learning mechanism. We feel as if we disappointed someone, or even ourselves. We know we messed up, and we hate what we did. The fact is, when you do something wrong, you did it. It may be hard to admit, but it's the truth. You did it, and that's okay, because you can learn from your mistake. This kind of shame can be painful, but it is pain that may teach us best.

The only shameful feeling that isn't okay is shame for characteristics that we cannot change.

Sometimes we let factors control our actions when we shouldn't. Sometimes these factors affect our heart and mind, which indirectly affects our actions. There are many things that can get to us and affect us. If this sounds like you, I don't blame you!

Sometimes, in the moment, something seems like the right thing to do, but later we look back in shame. You weren't trying to mess up--nobody <u>tries</u> to mess up. Yet, we all do, and we all feel ashamed of our past.

Maybe you messed up bad this time, and you're sitting here thinking, *what do I do?* Start by apologizing – to yourself, your friend, your teacher, your parent, or whoever you have affected by your actions. Whoever you let down, admit it and say you're sorry. If you are ashamed, you should feel sorry, so say it. Even if it changes nothing, you lose nothing from apologizing. It's always good to show you care.

You could think back through your past and feel ashamed of it for the rest of your life. Honestly, beating yourself up about it isn't bad at first, but only beat yourself up for a short while. One mistake doesn't define you. You must learn from it.

Get this self-blame and ridicule out of your mind, for everyone is a good person if they want to be--we just mess up.

Think back and ask why you truly did whatever you feel ashamed of. Ask yourself that question and admit the answer to yourself. Admit it and learn from it; that is all you can do after something has already been done.

The mess-up is behind you. You can't take back the words or actions. All you can do is be better in the future. Be better for the future. This is the single most important mindset to have when looking at your past. Don't let go of or hide from your past, or you are doomed to repeat it. I've tried, and it doesn't work very well. Instead, try to balance that bad action with one hundred good ones.

Being ashamed can teach us valuable lessons for the future, but it can also get out of hand. Remember that you are better than this one mess-up. You may hate what you did, so fix it. Be better, for the ones you love. You are better.

Don't spend time worrying about the past, because if you do, it consumes you. If it consumes you, it will become you and that mistake is, in fact, who you are. Be better than your past.

The reality is, you will mess up again at some point. When you do, you get to repeat the process all over again. Life is full of mistakes and setbacks. But you can rise above them every time and look for ways to better yourself so that the next time you don't make that same mistake. Admit it, accept it, and learn from it. That's the best thing you can do for yourself.

BETRAYED

It is easier to forgive an enemy than
to forgive a friend.
– William Blake

I t's very easy to feel betrayed, without someone even doing anything. And it's also not uncommon for someone to make a mistake and go behind your back. Both situations cause you to question a person and even your friendship, which is reasonable. Yet, you have to ask yourself, "Why did they do this?". If you can find that out, your next steps may become clear.

A betrayal by one of your best friends is one of the hardest things to experience. It may not even be one action, but maybe your friendship is changing, and you're left feeling betrayed. Like you put your trust into this relationship and now it's on a downhill slant.

Your mind may try to tell stories about what is happening – stories that probably are not true. Don't make assumptions and don't believe everything you might hear from others. Go to the source.

The best advice is talk to your friend and let them know how you are feeling. If they can't respect your feelings and have a mature conversation with you about it, perhaps you should be questioning the friendship.

Honest conversation is the most reliable path to a solution. Too often we build up walls around the truth because we are afraid of it. Honest talks break down these walls and reveals the truth in its full form. Just be 100 percent honest with your friend and invite them to hang out or go to lunch. You need to step back and reconnect with this friend. Disconnection is where betrayal thrives, and if you say nothing, you won't understand why the relationship is changing.

Usually, we feel betrayal from one action. One action can define a person from our perspective. They probably messed up, maybe even badly. This may even be a reoccurring thing. Don't let this action slide by. Don't let your voice go unheard.

Honesty is key to solving problems. Address the situation. Be understanding and fair. Do not let your anger decide if your friend is guilty.

Put yourself in their shoes. I'm not defending their wrongdoing, but rather defending the sure fact we all mess up in life. Greed, temptation, hate, anger, jealousy, confusion . . . these emotions can lead to bad actions. Actions that spread the feeling of betrayal--it is almost a natural occurrence.

Remember, it is not the someone's actions that define them, but rather their intentions. It is your job to decipher those intentions, based on honest discussion, and make decisions based on that.

Be forgiving. In the same way your heart may hurt, their heart may hurt too. Most people have pain in their hearts, and it is good to understand more than just intentions.

In any situation betrayal hurts, and it makes you build up walls around yourself. This can be one of the scariest things, when you feel as if you can't trust anyone anymore. Just know that there are good people out there. Do not isolate yourself, for that is where pain only grows.

It's easy to give up, to allow betrayal to change who you are, but don't let others' mistakes create your own mistakes. Find good, supportive people in your life, and never let them go. It is okay to let someone in, if their character and intentions are good. Don't let past betrayals limit you and keep you from worthwhile relationships.

BLAMED

*The misattribution of blame is one reason we
make the same mistakes over and over again.
We learn so little from experience because we
often blame the wrong cause.*
—Joseph T. Hallinan

For every bad thing in this world, we want there to be a cause. We always find someone to blame, and we often place false blame-on ourselves, but on others too. With all the negativity in this world, we just want someone to take it out on. Someone who we can pin all the bad karma on, and think it is all their fault and not ours.

People can also do this to us. Whether out of anger and hatred in their heart, misunderstanding, or hurt, they put all the blame on us. Sometimes we even start to believe them. Deep down, though, we know who is at fault, or if no one is.

For some reason, one of the hardest things for people to do is admit they messed up. We look back in guilt and disbelief within ourselves and struggle to own up to what we did. Everyone makes mistakes, sometimes badly, sometimes not, but we all mess up.

You might feel ashamed of what you did, but if you did it, admit it to yourself, then others. Whatever the mistake is, you know if you contributed to it or not. If you didn't do it, admit that too. Don't blame yourself for something you didn't do or can't control. This will ruin your self-confidence, for nothing.

Others may also try to blame you for things you haven't done. If this happens, listen to your heart. Deep down, you know what happened. If it wasn't your fault, don't blame yourself. If it was your fault, that's okay too, but don't let the guilt linger. Admit the mistake, apologize, and move on.

When we experience feelings resembling those of hostility towards someone or a circumstance, we look to place the blame upon a number of people and circumstances Casting blame is something we all do and sometimes we're lost as to who to blame. You don't need anything or anyone to blame for every miserable thing that happens. Bad things happen, people mess up, and you can't always do something about it. When you falsely blame someone or are falsely blamed yourself, it does zero good. Take out your frustrations on a pillow or in a healthy way, such as long run. You know what is true in your heart; listen to it.

If you try your best and make the best decisions you can, there is no reason to blame yourself. If you're not doing your best, then change it. When someone else is at fault, give them grace. Remember that everyone messes up, including you.

BORED

The cure for boredom is curiosity.
There is no cure for curiosity.
—Dorothy Parker

Boredom. Not a seriously life-changing, heart-crushing, or dangerous emotion. It's still not fun, but I can tell you exactly what to do. We often say, either to ourselves or someone else, that there is nothing to do. There's always something to do. That's what my dad says. He's right.

There are a lot of things you could be forced to do that are not fun, so be thankful for having the freedom to choose what you can do. Being bored is annoying, but preventable.

When I'm bored, it's often not that I have no options, but that none of them appeal to me. I sometimes even enjoy just sitting there and doing nothing for extended periods of time. It can be a good use of time when we need a break from the constant distractions in this world. It gives us time to be alone with ourselves and think. It can be healing as long as we don't get stuck on negative thinking.

When you feel unmotivated, think of it like getting out of bed. Once you get out of bed, you know it's time to work. Being bored is similar. If boredom happens during a forced activity, muster your positivity and try to enjoy the situation. Responsibilities and activities can be forced on us; we just have to enjoy them the best we can. We can't change the activity-so we change our perspective.

In any state of boredom, think of something you can do. I challenge you to not watch TV, play videogames, or surf the web. I challenge you to create human relationships and hang out with friends. Go live out your hobby and practice it. Perfect it.

If you're like me, maybe you feel self-disappointment and boredom. Then come up with an idea to change the world. It's ambitious, I know, but it doesn't have to be a huge act. Helping someone, reconnecting with an old friend, starting an online class, learning a new language on an app ... these things may not change the whole world, but they can help improve your world. Find something positive to do, and do it. It really is that simple.

Use your boredom to do something fun. Create a legacy, a good reputation for your name. Boredom is a huge advantage, because it's time that you have to do something. Do whatever you want, but do something good. You will feel happier than ever by helping others, creating something great, and being positive. This philosophy, combined with a little bit of free time, is where this book was written from.

BULLIED

*When a resolute young fellow steps up to the
great bully, the world, and takes him boldly
by the beard, he is often surprised to find it
comes off in his hand, and that it was only
tied on to scare away the timid adventurers.*
—Ralph Waldo Emerson

Dealing with bullying can be hard. Many bullies do mean things because they experience some of the negative emotions discussed in this book. Bullying is never okay. If you are being bullied, reach out to a trusted adult. Your mental and physical safety is priceless, so never be afraid to take action. If you're reading this and you feel you may be bullying someone, just don't. There may be some hatred in your heart, but bullying others is not the path you want to choose. Choose kindness, and spread it, even if it is not spread to you. If you're the one being bullied, please read this and be inspired to get help for yourself.

The following story comes from someone who was bullied.

"You're worthless, you know that, right?" "You don't belong, and you never will." "No one wants you here, so why don't you do everyone a favor and just die."

Imagine, having to go through your everyday life hearing people say stuff like this to you, just because they don't like you. From fifth to seventh grade, I was bullied. I didn't know what I did wrong or who I had hurt. I wanted the pain to stop. Every single day it felt like it got worse and worse.

I was in fifth grade when it all started. The "popular" group of girls never really liked me, and they thought it was a great idea to shun me, not include me, pretend I didn't exist, and I felt invisible. That sort of thing.

Yes, I was hurt and upset because all I wanted was to be friends with them, but they would just keep doing the same thing every day. Of course, I didn't tell anyone though. I was a fifth grader, and I didn't want to lose more friends and become a "snitch." So, I just faced it, every day. I wish I would have said something when it started, because little did I know how bad it would get.

Summer went by and school started again. Sixth grade. I had an open mind, thinking maybe they would change this year. Maybe they would like me. Oh, boy, was I wrong. Over the summer, more people had joined their "clique," and those people now hated me too. People didn't just pretend that I didn't exist; they made me hate that I did.

It started with just a push into a locker or getting tripped twice a week, not bad at first. But by the time we hit the middle of the school year, they were hating on me as a person, telling me I was ugly and fat and nobody liked me. I really felt worthless. Still, I didn't go to anyone or tell anyone except for my best friends, because I didn't want to make a huge thing out of it. I thought it would make everything worse.

Later that year, an app called Sarahah became trendy. It was an anonymous app where you could say anything you wanted and your name was not revealed. I decided to download it and create a profile. People were so mean. What they said still gets to me today. It's the reason I'm self-conscious, why I think people don't like me, and why I'm scared to trust.

They said things like "No one likes you" and "Go die, no one cares anyway." I didn't understand how people had the stomach to tell someone to end their life. It got to the point where there were so many negative comments that I cried and cried and cried every night.

One day, my friends had the smart idea of making me delete the app and taking a break. Still, I hadn't told anyone what was going on.

The school year ended, and summer passed by. Now I was in seventh grade. The year that would soon become the worst year of my life. The popular clique was still being so mean to me. Every day felt like a new day in which there was a new thing wrong about myself. I remember I would go to the bathrooms during some classes and just cry. I didn't know what I was doing wrong; I didn't know why they hated me. I just wanted a friend.

All year they made fun of me, called me worthless to this world, and pushed me around. Toward the end of the year, a guy came up to me and slapped me right across my face. He did it several more times that week, and I ended up with bruises on my face and a fear of things moving fast near my head.

That was my breaking point. I had finally had enough. I took myself and my best friend down to the office and straight to the vice principal. I told him what had happened and why there were bruises on my face. In fact, I told him the whole story. It felt good to finally get it all out, all the anger and sadness.

After telling the vice principal, he made the popular kids stop bullying me every day. Of course, they still hated me, and nothing went back to "normal," but life definitely got better.

As for the slapping incident, my parents heard about it and flipped out. The principals wanted to get rid of the matter as fast as possible. They called me down to the office and told me to "not tell anyone from other schools about this incident because it made our school look bad."

That made me angry, not because I was going to go out and tell the world my story, but because they were limiting my option to speak openly just for their reputation. I had kept my mouth shut for too long already, and now I had to do it again. By this time there was a week left in seventh grade, and I found out that was moving to a new school the next year. The year ended, and I haven't talked to any of the people from my old school since.

What I have learned is that I have something to offer, that true friends stick by you and support you through it all, and that if you cut all the toxic people out of your life, it makes life so much better.

If you or your close friends have gone through a similar situation, I encourage you to tell someone. Let them know what's happening. I know it's hard, and I know you think you're alone and no one cares, but there are people out there who can help you. There are so many people in this world who love and care about you and are ready to help you with whatever you have going on. Sure, everything doesn't go *poof* and change back to normal right away. It does take time, and you will hurt afterward, but I promise you, it gets better. You are never alone. You can do this.

CONFUSED

Anyone who isn't confused really doesn't
understand the situation.
—Edward R. Murrow

Life can be confusing. Crushes, relationships, homework, people, school, emotions ... it is all a bit confusing. Although there is a reason for everything that happens, those reasons are not always clear. We can easily look too hard for answers to already-answered questions. We're often confused about things with no clear answer. Perhaps that is the most confusing part. In this confusion, all you can do is try your best to come up with a clear answer - and be okay with knowing you may not always understand.

Confusion comes from the lack of a solution or answer to a problem, difficulty, or situation. Many things can be confusing. But any confusion can be cleared.

If you're confused about the reason for someone's action, or why they may be acting different in general, ask. You lose nothing from asking, but you gain the possibility of an answer.

If you're confused over a girl or guy, be patient and honest. I've been there. If you're confused over homework, help yourself. Check the textbook, ask a friend, look up how to do the problem, research, and learn. Some things, like your homework, have simple uniform solutions; realize and follow them. You must be willing to find the solution to your problem for it to be revealed.

Sadly, not all confusion drawn from problems has a cookie-cutter solution. Experiencing this just builds more confusion--on both the problem and the solution, because they are different.

In life you will face new situations all the time, some scary ones too, so you have to be ready for everything. But even when you're ready, you won't know exactly what to do in every single situation.

There will be shockers, and those bring confusion. When you find yourself in such a situation, try doing the following things:

- o Take some time to clear whatever emotions are affecting you if you're working through an emotionally confusing topic.
- o From a logical standpoint, begin to think about the problem. Start to form some ideas and decide the pros and cons of each. Consider the factors and impacts of your decisions.
- o When you come up with the best solution, go through with it, but be adaptable to the circumstances.

In the end, make the best decision you can. That's all you can do. You will face life, and with life comes complications. You just need to make the best decisions for both yourself and society.

Confusion comes from a load of things, so try to be prepared for dealing with it. Learn from your confusion and any failures that come as a result. Look for the best solution, and spend time thinking about it. This improves your chances of success, although it doesn't, unfortunately, secure them. And remember that sometimes you never find a clear answer, and that's okay too. Life is full of confusion, and all you can do is try to be prepared and remain flexible.

DEPRESSING

I was once thrown out of a mental hospital for
depressing the other patients.
—Oscar Levant

N ot to be confused with depression, which is a more serious issue. Some people always seem to be happy and just radiate positivity wherever they go. These types of people care and build you up, and being around them makes you feel great.

Some of us feel we are rather the opposite. We aren't mean but maybe negative, and negativity definitely spreads through and within us and can affect those around us.

The word "depressing" is something other people may call us; it may sound mean, but it's maybe one to listen to. I am often called "quiet" and "negative" by adults, including those closest to me. Right when I stopped denying them, and started listening is when I began to feel a lot happier within myself.

You may be depressing; it's okay. I understand that it can be hard to find and focus on the positive. But when you do, you will be rewarded in many ways.

Debbie Downer. Negative Nancy. These names are often put upon someone as another label for "negative." If you're someone who is very negative, on the outside or even the inside, the first step toward changing is to admit it. If you're in denial, nothing will change - it is just the way things are.

Admit to yourself that you may be someone who focuses on the negative aspects of life and that you may need to change. Nobody is born into this world with bitterness, and nobody likes being sad or negative.

If you feel you are depressing to be around, begin changing the way you think. If you think it, you say it, and if you say it, you are it. If you don't want to be a negative person, stop it at its source--the mind. It's hard to change one's own way of thinking, but not impossible.

First, hold yourself accountable for positive thoughts. If you begin thinking negatively, realize it and change your thought process. Try to understand why you may be having these thoughts. Maybe you are feeling insecure or jealous about, or simply have a bad attitude toward something. This is all normal, but look for ways to turn that into a reason to inspire yourself.

If you begin thinking positively and appreciating other people, you will feel better about the things you resent. Let your negativity go in a healthy way, such as a rant or deep talk with a trusted friend.

If your negativity is focused on people, remember that everyone in this world is alike. Wrongdoings are often not done on purpose. Try to give people the benefit of the doubt, and believe they are good. Try to see the good things in this world; they are out there. Your problems are real, but you have so many things to be happy about too. The moment you start focusing on these is when your negative ideology of life turns positive.

You want to be positive, because positivity spreads happiness. Start to understand that other people may struggle with negativity, just like you, and they need that positivity in their lives.

You will prosper if you begin thinking positive. Life is all about perception and how you view the world. The choice is yours. With negativity gone from your heart and mind, you will feel happy and lighthearted.

Understand what being depressing is like, and begin to help others. You can gain so much happiness from helping, inspiring, and empowering those around you. Don't be phony; be real, and choose to focus on the positive. For positivity is what fills our hearts with joy and the world around us with warmth.

DESPAIR

He who has never hoped can never despair.
—George Bernard Shaw

Despair is the loss of all hope. It is even worse than hopeless, because when we are hopeless, we often keep going, even if it seems pointless. The feeling of despair makes it very hard to continue hoping.

In the presence of despair, it is easy to stop and give up and continue in a downward spiral of hopeless thoughts until we hit rock-bottom. If we let despair build and build and do not try to rise from it early on, we can find ourselves in a load of trouble. Even in the moments when you feel life may be all despair, you can find reasons to hope and live. They already live inside you.

Despair often has a source: a negative situation or person. If you can help curb the source, or stop it completely, then obviously do so. Your happiness is priceless, and your voice is the most powerful weapon you have. So, if someone or something is bringing you down, you deserve the right to do something about it. Don't sacrifice your happiness for an unreasonable reason.

Yet we often feel despair for reasons unknown, non-existent, or self-caused. Sometimes you can't stop despair from starting, but you can keep it from consuming you. It may be hard, but many things seem impossible until you do them.

Without hope, reason, or purpose, negativity flourishes. You may beat yourself up over everything, blame your pain on yourself, and start a negative downfall.

I don't know what is causing you to feel despair. Maybe it's just one of those days. There are many things that could drag you down, but nothing reserves the right to do so. You deserve to be happy.

Right now, it may be all bad negative circumstances, thoughts, and people, but it won't be like this forever. If you keep pushing and going, it will get better. There are so many reasons to live--one of them is happiness.

Happiness may seem farfetched in your state of despair, but you can and will find it. Life events can cause despair that stays with us all the time, but keep pressing on.

We all experience hard times, yet only those who live through those difficult times get to the good ones. All the things that bring you down are worthless. Your worth is greater than all things in this universe. So, don't let worthless things ruin what you can do.

Despair requires a fight inside your heart. For some, it is a constant battle. For some, maybe it's just a realization you need to arrive at or one single battle. Whatever it takes, you will fight the good fight. You will find purpose in life, and you will clear yourself of negativity.

Life is too worthwhile and short to live with despair in your heart. Fight it and win. You are better than the things pulling you down. So, rise up and show them who you really are.

If you can't' seem to overcome your despair and you feel you can't go on with life, please get help! Tell a trusted adult, call a 24-hour hotline (1-866-4CRISIS), or seek counseling. Please do something to help yourself get better.

DISCOURAGED

One of the things I learned the hard way was
that it doesn't pay to get discouraged. Keeping
busy and making optimism a way of life can
restore your faith in yourself.
—Lucille Ball

There are many obstacles that can keep you from doing something: doubt, fear, limitations. But perhaps discouragement is the one thing that stops us by hitting us where it hurts us the most – our hearts. Lots of things can drag us down and make us feel discouraged.

Discouragement can make us question the point or existence of something. This discouragement can be direct or indirect. For example, direct discouragement is someone telling you not to do something for a reason. Indirect discouragement could be someone saying something or something happening that changes your thinking into self-doubt. Discouragement tries to stop you. The key word there is tries.

It is hard to go through with something when everywhere you turn, someone or something knocks you down. Direct discouragement and indirect discouragement are different, and both may affect you personally and differently from each other.

Direct discouragement comes from people. Now, if someone tells you not to run off the cliff, then don't run off the cliff. That's good advice. Yet, if someone questions your ability to accomplish a goal or task, learn something new, or do something important, that is different. When someone says you're too young, too old, too smart, too dumb, too ugly, too pretty, or whatever, don't listen.

You can do things you want to do. People may try to stop you. They might not believe in you and, frankly, that doesn't matter. All that matters is that you believe in yourself, and you go out there and follow your dreams. Now, if your dream is driving and you're under sixteen that's different. But hang in there until the right time comes!

Whether your dream is achievable or not, follow it. Everything is impossible until it isn't, and life is too priceless to not follow your dreams because someone else said you would never reach them. And if you don't reach them, there's nothing wrong with that, because at least you spent your time pursuing what you love. Do not waste your potential. Striving for your dream can be better than not trying at all.

Indirect discouragement can come from people too, and it affects how we react. A person may love singing, but if someone mentions that they aren't very good at singing, the singer's reaction determines if they are discouraged. The singer could be confident and not care, or they could be fragile and stop singing forever.

The fact is, it doesn't matter if you're good at singing. It doesn't matter if you are skilled. If you are passionate about something, follow that passion. Don't be discouraged by others. This is your life to live. You are not here so others can tell you exactly what you can and can't do.

Be aware. Not everyone who discourages you is set out to crush your dreams. Your dream should always be something you go after. Just know, reality doesn't often align with these dreams. Many people in your life may warn you that being a singer is hard. Especially if you're not an amazing singer. Your friends and family may discourage you from one thing, because they want to advise you to pursue a different plan. Take this discouragement as advice. Consider other's advice carefully and always be thinking of new goals, but you get to decide.

It is easy to get discouraged and stop. I get it. The problem is, no one changed the world by listening to the discouraging comments of others. If you love something and are passionate about it, then love that thing. Others may try to pick and choose your life for you, but when it comes down to it, it is your life.

DIFFERENT

In order to be irreplaceable one must
always be different.
—Coco Chanel

I f you're reading this chapter, you feel different, and you may assume different is a bad thing. Being different is something the world labels as "wrong." In this world, people often try to generalize others. We are lucky to live in a time of more diversity than ever, but we still can feel wrong or different on the inside. Different is different, that's it.

Uniqueness is something we should appreciate, especially in ourselves, as well as in others. You will never be the exact same person as someone else, and that is truly mind-blowing. No two people will ever be exactly the same, even twins. So why do we so often feel like we need to be like someone else? We feel we need to identify with a group or a person, and if we don't, we worry we will be left out.

Emotionally, we sometimes feel different in a way nobody understands. It can lead to loneliness. Society consistently fails to create an environment in which people can be themselves, and love themselves.

Physically, you may not think you're the best-looking, or that you have the perfect anything, in that sense. But in another sense, you are perfect in every single aspect because of the features that make up who you are.

We are all unique, different, and weird, and that is not a bad thing. That is an astonishing, amazing thing. You are you, and no one can change that. You have different strengths from your friends, your teachers, the leaders in your life ... different from anyone, so use your own skills.

You may feel that because you have different skills you are wrong. Or that no one will like the things you are amazing at. Take it from a fourteen-year-old boy who knows a lot about emotions, people will surprisingly respect your skills. They may act like it's lame or bad, but that's usually a cover for jealousy.

Embrace your gifts, embrace yourself, and embrace the things you can and will do. Don't let this world normalize you and take away from who you are.

Some of us may feel different on the inside. I know what that is like, to begin to isolate yourself emotionally because no one is like you. To suppress it because other people just don't quite get it. To hide aspects of yourself because you believe it is better to fit in that to stand out.

At the time, it doesn't even seem wrong. It isn't wrong. People are unique, but in many ways, they are all the same on the inside. We all have experiences in our pasts that shaped who we are, but deep down we are all the same. One day someone came to me, someone who was just like me. This indirectly taught me that we are all alike. We all are striving for happiness; we all have good and bad days. We all are good, deep down, if we choose to be, and are fueled by certain things.

People are different on the outside, but the same on the inside. We all want to connect and be known. It is one of the most beautiful things ever. It is the reason humans are above all else. These things we feel called emotions make us who we are, they bring diversity.

We all need the same things on the inside - love, compassion, acceptance - and on the outside, we should all embrace what makes us, us. All of us are virtually the same internally, but changed by the experiences we face. This concept of us all being the same is directly connected to empathy. Have empathy and be better than the people who ridicule you. Don't let anyone put you down for simply being who you are. Likewise, never put someone else down for being different, because all they're doing is the exact same thing as you, just in a different situation - being themselves. Different is so so right.

We all have differences that sometimes come down to personality. It's really differences in preferences and what motivates us as people. These differences are just that – differences. So, we should love ourselves, embrace our uniqueness and show an understanding for others' differences so they may show us compassion too.

DISAPPOINTED

*You may be disappointed if you fail, but you
are doomed if you don't try. —Beverly Sills*

Disappointment lies in the failure of our faith and trust. We all experience disappointment. Sometimes it's brief, and we move on. Other times the feeling drags on for weeks. For some, it's always nagging at us because we feel disappointed with ourselves.

Disappointment arises from the lack of expected results. It is produced from both others and ourselves. However, disappointment is merely our perspective when comparing outcomes and predictions. Disappointment is tough, but what follows can be great.

We often trust that things will hopefully work out, and when they don't, we feel discontent. It makes sense. We can put our trust in people too, and when they mess up, we feel disappointed. Yet people will always let us down if we come in with expectations – which they may not know anything about!

This feeling is one of those complex emotions, in which we aren't betrayed or heartbroken, or even especially sad. It's important to recognize disappointment, however, because it can lead to other emotions that will affect your well-being.

When you feel disappointed in something or someone, try to focus on the good in your life. Look at the people you love. Look at all the things you have. The fact is, you are alive, and you were created. When we put these thoughts foremost in our mind, we realize this small disappointment should not stop us from taking advantage of the luckiest thing ever--life itself.

You may have flipped to this chapter because you do feel that nagging feeling of disappointment. Disappointment is a small barking dog. It doesn't shut up. It is loud and the longer it goes on, the more accustomed you get to the noise, but just like the little barking dog, you never truly get rid of the noise, unless it is stopped completely.

When we feel disappointed, we're not mad or angry, but we feel sorry for ourselves. We feel discontent with the situation. Yet, this is usually a self-made problem. When you feel sorry for yourself, instead of wallowing in it, use that feeling to do better. If your life is not what you want it to be, change it. Or at least try to.

Many of us are teens, and we can't just easily do that, but you can control what YOU do. So, get out there and use your disappointment as a reason to be better. Think of those things that make you happy, that you are lucky to have.

Stop trying to control things that are out of your control. Try not to have expectations that can't be met – this brings constant disappointment. Instead focus on what you can control and change within yourself.

Disappointment can be tough to handle and often leads to something much worse –anger or despair. We can stop it at the source and transform it. Fuel yourself, and don't let life and outside factors get you down. If we let disappointment define us, we think we are a disappointment. So, prove yourself and everyone else wrong.

DOUBTFUL

The whole problem with the world is that
fools and fanatics are always so certain of
themselves, but wiser people so full of doubts.
—Bertrand Russell

Many things can shake our trust, hope, and faith. Small things can make us feel skeptical about certain aspects of our life--this is the presence of doubt. Doubt isn't the same as being afraid, because you can feel doubt without fearing the outcome.

Instead, you feel worried over a promise, commitment, or expected results. Maybe this feeling of doubt is completely reasonable, due to your past experiences. This world may fill you with doubt, and trustees may sometimes fail, but doubt can kill the joy in any situation. What does the outcome matter if you do not enjoy the time leading up to it?

If you're doubtful over the future, the present will be overshadowed by this everlasting sense of approaching failure. I know it is easy to overthink about the future, and even wonder why you are doing something, what the purpose of it is. But I challenge you to think about your questions while not overthinking them. Have faith in what you are doing.

It's so easy to wander through life with a negative lens over everything you do. This is a straight-up fun killer. It's also easy to doubt everything you do, doubt your future, doubt yourself, doubt others--in fact, it is too easy. If you have faith in your future, yourself, and others, you will see that the outcome doesn't necessarily matter; the experience does, and it should be fun.

You've probably heard this saying: Life is a journey, not a destination. Too many of us hear this, think about it for a moment, and then allow it to fade from our mind, instead of letting it really sink in.

If you're filled with doubt, you are focused too much on the destination, on what is to come. I too can get caught up in the future, and it scares me; it fills my heart with doubt. We all sometimes need to refocus on the present. Live in the present, and make decisions for your future.

Like in a court case, we should consider a person innocent until proven guilty. If their action can be interpreted two ways, choose to believe the most respectful one. Life isn't about holding grudges, so give the right people the right second chance. You may get hurt, and people may break your trust, but it'll be okay in the end. If you spend every waking moment worrying about a bad outcome, then you ruin the journey and sometimes the destination.

At one point, you may look back on the doubtful life you have been living and see all the good experiences you passed up, and then, when it may be too late, learn to trust in that instant.

I know it can be hard to trust people. Especially those who fail you repeatedly. But it's good *for you* to trust people. There are times when it's good to be doubtful, such as if someone is pushing for a bad decision. Bu also remember that doubt can ruin the present, and it doesn't necessarily help your future.

Trust yourself to make the right decisions, and trust others, slowly but surely. When you do this, life will be filled with optimism. It won't be without setbacks, and while you can steer along the journey, and you can't always control the destination. That is part of the fun – sometimes the destination will be a pleasant surprise.

EMBARRASSED

If you're never scared or embarrassed or hurt,
it means you never take any chances.
—Julia Sorel

Everyone feels embarrassed about different things, and everyone experiences embarrassment differently. This directly correlates to self-confidence--the more confidence you have, the less you care about other people's opinions.

In today's world, it's very easy to have low self-confidence and feel embarrassed over every little flaw or mistake. We all can feel this way, and it just radiates negativity. It is easy to be broken down, to feel as if your every imperfection or every imperfect decision will define who you are.

You're right--these things do define who you are, but in the best way possible. The existence of your imperfections is the only reason you are "perfect," because there is perfection in embracing your imperfections.

You may be embarrassed about things you can't control, from a pimple to the house you live in. Yet, these things are not on you; nothing you did made you deserve these perceived shortcomings. There's no need to be embarrassed, because these things are not your fault; you should embrace what you have and respond with a proud voice. There is always someone who is worse off.

Confidence ... it scares people. When someone calls you out, with the intention of ridiculing you, the easy solution is to accept it. Some things can't be changed, and denying things doesn't mean they didn't happen. By feeling embarrassed, you give in. I challenge you to instead stand up proud and accept who you are. Accept who you are on the inside, and begin to voice it on the outside.

You may also be embarrassed by mistakes you've made. This is completely normal. We all mess up, and it is okay to regret what you have done. If it was something bad, use your embarrassment to bring change to your future actions.

You can't always fix what you have done, but you can make better choices in the future and remind people of the good in you.

When you feel embarrassed, it's also a good time to practice accepting that you messed up and learning from your mistakes, instead of making excuses and playing it off.

The past is a collection of facts – it is unchangeable. It is also undeniable. We all have looked back and asked *Why did I do that?* Just know that it doesn't necessarily matter why. While it is good to understand your thinking behind what you did, know sometimes out thinking is wrong for a variety of reasons. Don't beat yourself up too much. What matters now is that you accept the fact that it happened, not the fact you did it. More importantly, can you learn from it?

The greatest people in history were the ones with a fully opened mind, who were not afraid to be embarrassed of their faulty actions (and learn from them). Thomas Edison is a great example. This man failed over 3,000 times before successfully creating a light bulb. In fact, he did not even consider his attempts to be failures, just 3,000 ways that it didn't work. This mindset is a great example to those who are embarrassed over their missteps.

The greatest and happiest people had life figured out. They learned that it isn't about feeling bad about things who make you who you are, because those are just part of an interesting journey. Life is about doing things that fill you up, about being yourself and loving yourself. Through this acceptance, all other forms of joy flow without tension.

EMPTY

In a full heart there is room for everything,
and in an empty heart there is room for
nothing. —Antonio Porchia

O n the outside, we may seem fine. We may go to school and for seven or
eight hours a day express this sort of happiness. We seem happy, but it's
a stretch. On the inside, we feel close to nothing. We feel empty. Life isn't
supposed to go our way, because it hasn't yet. Life is just an endless cycle, and for
what? We've thought about life in every way, until there are none left to think
about. We still have found no meaning for life, and no feelings for ourselves. Life
becomes pointless, and as it does, we begin to feel pointless too.

I can't argue; life can be repetitive. We do the same thing five days a week, with
a two-day break after every fifth day. Through these cycles, months and years go
by. Our problems aren't fixed, our happiness is dwindling, and our faith that
something good will happen dissipates. We haven't seen the reward for putting in
the work of surviving life, and so we begin to think there is no reward. Life isn't
good, in fact; it's just something we do.

Honestly, that's very easy to think. When we think this way, we begin to look
around and see other people who are thriving. So, we put the blame upon ourselves.
We begin to feel too small to change our lives, and we simply accept the fact life
isn't the way we want it to be.

It's not easy to believe without seeing. Sometimes you can't see your own
potential, but that doesn't mean it's not there. You probably just haven't been
given your major breakthrough, opportunity, or chance yet.

You may feel you're not worthy, but you are. You will go through life every day,
and one day your chance will come. You will take it.

Life gives every bird a worm, but it doesn't put it in the nest. The bird has gone
to find it. Do not go through life just waiting for something big to happen though.

You have a lot to be happy about. Is a good meal a Nobel Prize? No, but that doesn't take away from the reality that it is a good meal.

You are not defined by the fact you haven't done this amazing thing in life yet, nor are you the reason for it. Regardless of where you are, there are so many great things about your life and yourself. Find those things and love them.

Life is worth living to the fullest, if you decide it is. And life will become worth living if you fill your emptiness with faith in yourself, the world, and the future. Just like bowls, we may be made empty, but we were put on this planet to be filled and serve a purpose.

Life can feel pointless. You may feel empty. It's easy to give up, and it's hard to keep going. But if you keep going, and love doing it, you will soon find that life does have a purpose. Go through life with a joyful attitude. For happiness will plant a seed in your heart, one that will grow and fill that emptiness. But the only person who can plant that seed is you, and you must plant it with faith. Take a leap, and don't look back.

(LIKE A) FAILURE

Many of life's failures are people who
did not realize how close they were to
success when they gave up.
—Thomas A. Edison

Success is the ability to go from one failure to
another with no loss of enthusiasm.
—Sir Winston Churchill

S tandards are either met or not. When we meet the standards, it is success; when we don't it is failure. Standards can be set by people who are considered more powerful than us, but they can also be set by ourselves, parents, friends, or society. Honestly, there are many standards we are required to meet throughout life. Falling short of these standards is summed up in one word: failure.

It insane how often life deteriorates us because we do not meet the expected standards. All over the world, your success is determined by your ability to meet other's standards. In school, we are in a classroom for seven hours, where we must follow specific directions, be quiet, and sit still. They call it education, but it seems more like generalization. Through this daily experience, many kids feel like a failure every day because they are forced into something that isn't who they are.

It is the concept of failure that has stopped us from questioning failed practices. So, let us start by questioning the idea of failure.

What is failure? Who defines your failures? Failure is missing the bull's-eye, but maybe we aren't all archers. You do not define failure, even if you think you do –you don't. You are influenced by others who have defined failure for you.

True failure only derives from one thing: not trying. Everything else is success; it just may not be what you, or someone else, expected. If you feel you can do

47

better, or that you messed up, learn from it and do better the next time. That is all you can do. There is no other way to put it: all you can do is try.

When you try your very best, with no excuses, there is no failure--only success. Try new things, and work smart too, but don't go through life believing you are failure because you don't align perfectly with modern standards.

Set your own standards and your own goals. Be ambitious, and when you don't reach them, celebrate the fact that you tried. Don't give up, but recognize and reward your own effort just as much as "successful" results.

Success is the way you choose to view it. Lately, I've seen the potential of people wasted because the education system wants us all to be the same. Put every comma in the same place, read the same article, do your math homework every night, get to school, read your textbook, don't be late, don't talk when the adults are talking ... and if you break any of these, you are a failure. It's a system of power, and the idea of failure is created for us not to challenge this power. Your success is different from the way people try to portray it.

In this weird world, we can feel failure in all areas of life. I get it. You are not the failure though; the world has failed to recognize your strengths. If you are the worst at schoolwork, but art is your strength and passion, it doesn't mean you're a failure. It means you are a successful artist. I fit this world's generalization, but the only real success I've ever had is the words on this page.

If you haven't found your skills yet, find them. Stop going through the world's cookie cutters and be yourself. Try new things – find what you are good at and what makes you happy, and be that. This is the only way you be truly successful.

FORGOTTEN

There's an old saying about those who forget
history. I don't remember it, but it's good.
—Stephen Colbert

irst things first. People our age don't forget (maybe older people do); they don't move on. People remember other people, especially the ones they care about. So how come we can still feel like everybody has moved on? To the point we think people do not remember us. Why do we sit back and let ourselves be ... forgotten?

People get busy, life happens. Summer brings free time, the rejuvenation or start of a major friendship. Everything is going great--best friends, yay! Then life moves along: responsibilities, work, school . . . we get busy and caught up in the commotion. We feel forgotten when the friendship begins to go through a hard time, and we blame ourselves. Trust me, this friend still cares about and can't forget you.

Friendships often experience a disconnect, one that can feel permanent, or one that can be just a break, a gap that can be filled. If you truly care about someone, you will put aside fear and other factors to overcome the separation. It's common to drift apart, but in times of change or busy seasons, we must persevere and stake down the friendship. Doing so is very simple and just requires two things: time and effort.

It doesn't matter how busy you are. If you want the connection, if you want to re-strengthen your relationship, you will make time. Talk to your friend; check in on them every day. It may be hard, and it might not be much, but all it takes is one conversation. One conversation a day. Talk to your friend and be honest.

Life can get the best of us, and it's easy to let friendships move down on our list of priorities. This doesn't mean you've been forgotten or replaced; it just means you might need to put some effort into the bond. It doesn't mean you've been passed by and aren't needed--it doesn't mean you don't matter to your friend.

People don't forget us, but a reminder doesn't hurt. We all know what it's like to feel swallowed by the rising tide of responsibilities. But falling out of touch doesn't mean you're forgotten. Nor is it anybody's fault. But if the friendship is important to you, don't sit back and let it happen. Tell them.

There are times within my own life that my friendships fade. It can be sad, but life happens. Today, most of us can text a friend, and so that is what I do. Just a simple conversation can help me reconnect with a friend. People can be understanding and will be understanding if they are your friend. Just reach out, you lose nothing from it.

Time and effort: two simple things, and if you care about being remembered, set fears about being vulnerable aside, and invest in your friendships.

Sometimes due to changes in yourself or your interests, you may grow apart. That's okay too. Understand that there are seasons in life where friendships change and losing one may open the door for a new friendship yet to be.

FRUSTRATED

Laughter and tears are both responses to
frustration and exhaustion. I myself prefer to
laugh, since there is less cleaning up to do
afterward. —Kurt Vonnegut

Frustration is the mad side of disappointment —it's what we feel when things don't go our way and we get angry. Sometimes we don't know what exactly what we are mad about; that doesn't matter though – we're just upset. Life brings unexpected outcomes. So many things aren't going to go the way you expected, or the way you hoped. When this happens, we can fill up with anger, rage, and resentment.

We most often feel frustrated when we hit a block. Things didn't go our way, and, in addition, we are stuck. We might resort to unhealthy things to relieve our stress. Dealing with frustration is hard, and it can cause us to crash and burn.

Life definitely puts us through challenges and places roadblocks on our path to success. The road still leads to success though, and although there are many ways to overcome these roadblocks--through, around, over, under--we must pick the best option.

You won't feel frustrated if you know what to do. The problem is, we don't. The first step to finding your way is to step away, step away from what you are doing, and look. Look at what is stopping you and why it is stopping you. Before you let anger run high and patience run low, calm yourself. When we are calm, solutions become clearer. Whatever your problem is, it's not the end of the road. It never is. You can and will get around this hardship. We must let our decisions be made with good intentions and not for time's sake.

Once you have stepped away and considered your problem, your opportunity stopper, think about your solutions. As I mentioned before, there may be many ways to go around this--or straight through it. This is when we must decide what's best and what actually works. Try to remain calm through this period. Begin to gather yourself and be purposeful about getting it done and solving your problem. Sometimes the solution contradicts what we may think would be right, but use this as a learning experience and not a reason for more frustration.

It's important we don't let frustration stop or control us. This can build up hatred and makes us want to give up. Amidst the trial, lies a key to success, and we must find this key. Frustration is not that key--all it achieves is anger and it changes who you are in the moment.

We mustn't ever lose ourselves to a silly thing. We are the greatest thing to ever happen to ourselves. You will get through this problem, and you will get through it brilliantly, and when you do, remember why you did.

GRUMPY

*One of the very first things I figured out about
life...is that it's better to be a hopeful person
than a cynical, grumpy one, because you have
to live in the same world either way, and if
you're hopeful, you have more fun.*
—Barbara Kingsolver

The circumstances of life can so often sour our mood. I encourage you to read this with a learning mindset. When we feel a combination of anger and annoyance, in this state lies grumpiness. When we wake up after a short night of sleep or come home after a long day of work, we often feel grumpy. Grumpiness can also be caused by feeling drained of things like trust, patience, and faith. It can affect what we say and do in a negative way.

It's hard to simply snap out of it, because when we are grumpy, we are also content with our feelings —we do not care because we think our emotion is justified by the circumstances. The world may annoy you constantly, but life is 90 percent how you react to it. Be wise enough to realize you are better than your grumpy self.

With a grumpy mindset, we are often short-tempered and self-centered. We want everything to go our way, and when it doesn't, we get mad. We don't even think about how our words and actions can affect others. Through our frustration with the situation, we often resort to this feeling just so we can get through our day. We become grumpy because we want to shut everyone out, but we know we must go on with normal life proceedings.

Being grumpy comes from the draining of ourselves, and life can drain us. So, I challenge you to take time to truly rejuvenate yourself, so you don't just life live but enjoy it.

When you're grumpy, sometimes you don't notice it yourself, but someone else will tell you. Instead of allowing this to make you grumpier, listen and try reasoning with yourself. <u>Yes, I'm grumpy because of my day at school or my day at work; it just really got me agitated and I'm kind of done.</u> Well, then take some time to be done. Whatever your favorite hobby is or a calming mechanism you may use, do that.

You don't want to be grumpy and no one around you wants you to be grumpy. This attitude radiates negativity, but if we start to recognize it when it happens and deny it at its source, we won't feel grumpy. Ask yourself: Is the thing that is annoying me life-changing? If it isn't, then you're in this bad mood for absolutely no reason.

Like the Snickers commercial says, "You're not you when you're hungry," the same goes for grumpy. We want to pursue being happy and being a good, positive person always. So, if something is changing your mood, and you can do something about it, then do it. Take a short break from what you're doing, and reconnect with yourself. Release the tension inside in a healthy way. That short amount of time spent taking care of you will help you live out the rest of your day more productive and happier.

You are better than whatever is holding you back. It takes self-will and realization to say no to grumpiness and let positivity shine on your day instead, but the effort is with it. For that sun will grow many flowers.

GUILTY

*Hard though it may be to accept, remember
that guilt is sometimes a friendly internal
voice reminding you that you're messing up.*
—*Marge M. Kennedy*

B efore I begin, I think it's necessary to tell you that it is going to be okay. Guilt usually comes from a mistake. We make mistakes, and when we see the consequences of those mistakes, we feel guilty. In fact, you can really <u>feel</u> guilt--it hurts your heart, your stomach, even your soul.

I like to think we have developed the feeling of guilt to prevent us from doing bad things. If you think about it, it's amazing that we feel pain from doing something wrong. It certainly doesn't feel amazing though. We often feel the most guilt when we have yet to admit what we did or are doing. Even once you do admit your mistake, guilt still lingers. It is one of the hardest emotions to deal with.

But remember it is going to be okay. You rarely feel guilty for nothing. So, you most likely did mess up, if we are being honest here. You may continue feeling guilty for a while, even after admitting to and apologizing for your mistake. You may find that something triggers your guilt until after you have fully moved on. But all you can do is not continue to blame yourself for things that happened in the past, and do better in the future.

If you're feeling guilty for something you are keeping in the dark, it may be time to admit that secret. If you don't, you may never clear the guilt from your soul. Now, if what you did is already out and the guilt lingers, think about ways to make up for what you did. We all mess up, so try your best to reconcile it. Know, however, that you may not always be able to completely fix it, unfortunately.

Understand that what you did has consequences. I hate to be the bearer of bad news, but you may have to live with those consequences. Although you should try to fix what may be broken, some things are unfixable. If that is the case, admit it and don't waste your energy. Realize things also get better with time.

People all mess up, and if you disappointed someone, remember that time heals wounds of the heart. Be patient, and don't be too hard on yourself. You messed up, so what? We all do. If you can't fix it, you can learn from what you did, and the pain should fuel you to be better.

You won't ever fully stop making mistakes, but you can certainly strive to avoid them. Understand what you did, the effects and consequences, and learn from them. Fix it, if you can, give it time to heal, and accept it.

We all feel guilty at some point. If something you are doing is constantly filling you with guilt, consider what the best steps are. Guilt will chip away your heart if left untouched. You can't always cure it all the way, but guilt is there to slap you in the face and transform you into a better person. Guilt is there to bring change for the better.

HATED

Sadly, we look around today and see a world filled with hatred. Maybe it's perspective, because I like to think that the good in this world outweighs the bad. Maybe it's because we don't just see it, we spread it. Sometimes it feels as if all this hatred in the world is aimed at us. As if the world in general decided one day it didn't like us.

Maybe the world even gives a reason, but there is no reason for hatred--ever. This knowledge doesn't help us feel any less hated though, because we too often agree. When it feels like the world, our friends, and even our family all hate us, soon enough, we hate ourselves too.

There will always be people who hate others, people who point out your mistakes and blow out of proportion those mistakes. All because they don't want people to see what is wrong with them, and the mistakes they have made.

Maybe you did mess up badly. If so, admit it, and apologize. We all make mistakes; once you have apologized, try to make up for what you did. Work toward being a better person. Nothing can change what you did. It's not easy to accept, but with time and a will, you can give people a reason to love.

Some may argue that we don't have to do anything wrong to feel hated, that it is a sad reality of our lives. People have so much pain in their hearts that it turns to anger, and then to hatred. Many people who feel hated do not know where it comes from. They begin to think everyone hates them, when they don't.

When we begin to fill ourselves with hatred, it becomes who we are. All we feel is hatred toward everyone, and it feels all we receive is hatred in return. It's hard to hate a nice, genuine person. So be one--be a person who builds others up, instead of tears them down. Cure the hatred in your own heart by spreading love.

This world may fill us with hatred-sometimes it's all we see, hear, and feel--
and we focus on the negativity, which makes it very easy to hate, and sometimes
very hard to love. Hate brings few risks, but love brings too many.

Love fixes problems; positivity fixes problems. So why do we strain away from
it? Because it's hard to go against the grain. To be different from others. What
makes you different doesn't make you wrong. If you feel hated, then love others.
For you can change both the way people think of you and the way people think of
themselves.

HEARTBROKEN

You've got to learn to leave the table When
love's no longer being served.
—Nina Simone

There's no doubt heartbreak sucks. I write these words a mere eight hours after going through it. On any level, we cannot comprehend this type of loss. Many have tried. Many have written hit songs and albums based entirely on this emotion.

You feel heartbroken when the person you care about most says they don't care about you anymore. This experience isn't easy for anyone, and it can build up so much resentment and bitterness inside. You love, but also hate the person who hurt you. You cry because you don't know what else to do. It's hard.

Heartbreak is also unique to each individual and experience. Sometimes we just want to take a baseball bat and smash something, so that object too can feel what it's like to get crushed. Sometimes we just want to cry and eat ice cream and cry some more. We blast sad love songs because we want to feel like we're not crazy.

You are not crazy; we all go through heartbreak, and it sucks. It's one of the worst things to live through. To make matters worse, there is no set-in-stone solution to this feeling. For all of us, it will be different. Yet, like any emotion, we cannot let this sad experience limit us.

It is perfectly reasonable to cry--that's love and, more specifically, the loss of it. You may need hours or days to yourself to sit there and cry. That's okay! There is nothing wrong with that. At some point, though, you have to rise above. This isn't easy; for some of us it can be depressing.

It is okay to feel heartbroken, but don't let that change who you are. If it didn't work out, maybe it is not meant to be. From a guy who just had his heart broken, I can still say this.

If your ex broke up with you, that's on them. You may feel like it is your fault. Maybe you messed up and now it's over. Or maybe the relationship had just run its course. That's the thing, though, it's over. It's no one person's fault. Life happens, the world isn't perfect and so many things can mess up a relationship. Do not think you're not good enough, because you are always more than good enough.

Somewhere in this world is a person, the person meant to be with you. Someone who is perfect for you and will care for you. Somewhere out there, there is a destiny waiting for you. It's not necessarily going to show up at your feet. Somewhere out there, your future waits.

Pursue your own happiness. Don't let some stupid breakup mess you up. Don't let it keep you from becoming the person you can become. Have your days of sorrow, but when it's time, prove to yourself that you're good enough.

I promise you, you are. Love is love, and soon enough you'll feel it again. For now, have some fun.

HESITANT

While one person hesitates because
he feels inferior, the other is busy
making mistakes and becoming superior.
—Henry C. Link

People have a certain indicator of when to do or not do something--it's called discretion. When we want to do something but there are certain consequences and sacrifices that come with it, we may be hesitant.

Decision making is hard, because one decision can have so much impact. One decision can affect the future, even if you're not considering that. Worry about these impacts is what is makes you hesitant. Hesitancy can be helpful, like if you are about to do something stupid or dangerous. But it can also hold us back from doing great things. Hesitation is complicated, so it's best to identify where it derives from.

If you're feeling hesitant, ask yourself why. The reason you are hesitant is what will lead you to the best decision. For example, if you are hesitant because you could get hurt or the thing you're considering is dangerous, look at the example of others. What you are about to do has probably been done before, so look at how it impacted those people to decide whether you should go through with it. Above all else, your safety and life is worth more than anything.

On the other hand, if you are hesitant because you're only worried about what others will think, just do it. Concern over others' opinion of you is so minor compared to your potential.

Above all else, hesitation comes from worry. This is a good thing to think about, because experiencing worry or fear is okay. Hesitation can help you make your decision. Think about why you are worried or afraid, and ask yourself: is it worth it? Are your worries going to come true? If they do, is it really the end of the world, or is it a personal sacrifice?

Hesitation is a checkpoint for us to consider our actions beforehand. Every decision has an impact. There is risk and reward with everything. They are many ways things could play out, and there are pros and cons to each of those ways. I say this not to confuse you, but to get you thinking. In times of hesitation, it's good to know that we make the best decision we can. So, think about it and trust yourself. Don't let others impact your decisions.

Hesitation can save us, or it can be a thing we pass by and it doesn't save us. In any time of hesitation, consider what you are doing. Use that tool in your brain--discretion. There are many decisions you could make, and it is up to you to decide if it's worth it.

Your decision after hesitation can impact you negatively or positively. Don't always be too hesitant. It is good to take a leap of faith once in a while. You may make the wrong decision, but it is good to take risks. Life is short and confusing, one of the best ways to enjoy it is be smart but risky.

You will mess up sometimes and make some wrong decisions too. We all will. Don't let this discourage you, though. Instead, learn from it. No matter what, pick a path and stick with it unless your discretion tells you otherwise. It's okay to change your mind. Before you make a decision, search yourself to see if you have any hesitations. Make sure you are confident in your decision. If you carry hesitation into everything, you can be held back from anything.

HOPELESS

There are no hopeless situations; There are only people who have grown hopeless about them. —Clare Boothe Luce

Hope gives us a reason to keep going. It makes us excited. It tests us, but it carries us too. Hope, even in its smallest amount, gives us belief. Belief in what is to come. The outcome is improved, because when we believe, we work. This is great to hear, but it seems like just a dream for many and a reality for only few.

When we go through life scared, timid, and unconfident, or when things do not go our way, we may begin to feel hopeless. That feeling can transfer into everything we do, and our lives in general. This virus kills hope. Without hope, purpose dissipates, and sadness overwhelms the heart.

In anyone's life, there will be tests, and some are tests you will fail. We sometimes test each other or test the world, and it too fails us. There will no doubt be hardships and trials in our lives. Times where we see nothing good, where we can't catch a break. It builds up, and we begin to think our lives will always be like this. Like this ditch we are stuck in will be one we can't escape. We lose the hope of getting out, of better things. We accept things as they are and go through life on autopilot, because we have to.

Everyone experiences these feelings at times, and it can seem as if it's the end, as if it's the norm. The only thing that will get you out of that ditch is the desire to, the will to. It's not easy, but if you regain your hope, your belief, you can prosper.

Now, exactly how you do this varies from person to person and situation to situation. If this is one bad night, then find one reason to keep going, if for no one other than yourself, your future, your potential. It is all out there, but you have to go get it.

I believe in you, but you have to believe in yourself. Life will test you and fail you, but this is only a reason to work harder. A reason to prove everyone--and sometimes yourself--wrong.

Maybe this isn't just one bad night. Maybe every night is another bad night. I have no idea what kind of ditch you're stuck in, what your problems are, or what is holding you back. But I don't need to, because everything can seem hopeless when something goes wrong. It is incredibly hard to see the good that the future holds when the bad days and nights pile up.

If you're in this place now, take a second recognize and acknowledge it. Maybe you've never admitted what is sucking the hope out of you. Whatever is testing you, admit it now. You may not be able to do this alone, so if you need help, get some. Sometimes, the aftermath is ten times worse than the bad things that happened, because it stops you from appreciating the good things and times that are happening too.

In times of bad, be sad, be mad, feel bad-but don't forget that this is a reason to fight, to do better. This world may hurt you; those people may try to stop you. Believe in yourself, and believe in everything you do-every single thing. Don't feel hopeless, because there is hope inside you, deep down in your heart. Right now, you may not feel it, but it is there and it's calling to you.

Hope will carry you when life tests you, and even when you fail. In tough times, it's easy to make it more difficult on ourselves. The hard part is saying no. The hard part is hope.

Hope lives in our hearts, and everyone has a good heart. This world may beat that heart, but deep down we are good people, people who need each other.

Your life isn't pointless. You will give it purpose. Work hard through the hard times, and life will be as great as you make it. When we lose hope, we lose opportunity. That's what the evil in this world wants. Fight it. Hope is in you. Find it and use it. It's never easy, but the best things aren't.

HUMILIATED

Life makes fools of all of us sooner or later.
But keep your sense of humor and you'll at
least be able to take your humiliations with
some measure of grace. In the end, you know,
its our own expectations that crush us.
—Paul Murray, Skippy Dies

There are a few reasons you could feel humiliated, but I think many of them are covered in other chapters. The humiliation we talk about here is humiliation of who you are. When someone teases you, you feel this way, or you could feel humiliated in fear of rejection or feeling different. Many of these insecurities or differences are just the person we are.

The most humiliating part of humanity is that people are so quick to point out these insecurities and put others down for their own confidence or enjoyment. We must stop this by not letting it affect us and not treating others this way. It's a two-birds-with-one-stone outcome. We destroy hurtful people's source of entertainment and boost our own confidence at the same time.

Many people in the world will try to humiliate you, especially in front of your peers, usually because they lack their own confidence. So, they tear down others to feel better about themselves. If this is you, stop, because you won't find true happiness or confidence by putting others down. It may feel like happiness, but it's just a cover-up. Knowing that people will try to humiliate you for anything (and I mean anything!), you have to be prepared for how to respond. There are people who would try to ridicule you for curing cancer, simply because of their own jealousy. You cannot stop these trolls, but you can take away their power by ignoring them.

Instead, listen to yourself and people you have earned your trust and respect. If someone tries to humiliate you for something that makes you unique, embrace that uniqueness. One thing I do is make fun of myself in front of others. It seems a bit ridiculous, but it works. It makes me feel more open about what I'm worried about, and if someone else says something, it doesn't hurt because I've already said it.

There are many strategies for not feeling humiliated, but the sum is to not allow yourself to feel this way. It's a choice you can make.

Don't waste your precious time worrying about what others say or think about things that make you who you are. You are perfect, and if you're humiliated about any part of yourself, admit it right now. Admit it, and then throw it away.

Now, you aren't <u>really</u> perfect--no one is, and no one can be. You will never be enough for some people, so judge yourself by their measure. Be enough for you. You will find happiness in not changing yourself, but embracing yourself. It's not easy, but if you do have this mindset, what others say will just encourage you. When people try to humiliate me, I find strength in the fact that I don't have to act like them just for my own happiness.

Remember, no matter what you achieve, some people will try to drag you down. Sadly, the world feeds on mistakes, mess-ups, imperfections, insecurities, and weaknesses. The best defense is admitting them, learning from them and embracing them and loving them. It isn't easy, and it certainly is a fight, but it's one that, if you learn to win, will result in many rewards.

You are you. You are perfectly you. The truth that no one is perfect is the one reason why we all are-in our own special ways.

HURT

*I have learned now that while those who
speak about one's miseries usually hurt, those
who keep silence hurt more.* —C. S. Lewis

There are two sides to every human experience. Positivity and negativity, happiness and sadness, peace and war. Emotional pain lies in the negative counterparts to the essentials of happiness and well-being. To be hurt is to feel pain, whether mental, emotional or physical.

The first time you felt pain as a child, you almost certainly cried. Maybe even today, pain still brings tears. Maybe today, you have learned to hide the tears and keep the pain inside. You will be hurt emotionally--it is a guaranteed sacrifice of living. You just have to learn how to deal with the pain.

Lucky enough, if you get a cut or scrape it heals all on its own. You don't have to think about it, or do anything but bandage the wound to help your body do all the work.

Emotional pain, on the other hand, left untouched, grows. If you leave emotional pain alone, or just put a metaphorical Band-Aid over it, it doesn't simply go away. It sits there, and affects everything you do. It messes with your heart, your hope, your trust, your happiness-all is clouded with a lining of pain.

Pain must be dealt with, not forgotten, and it may be very hard. If there is something or someone in your life hurting you constantly, get rid of that thing or person. You don't deserve constant pain. I know sometimes it isn't as simple as just letting go, but sometimes it can be. You never deserve that pain. Help yourself and advocate for yourself.

Even if you aren't in constant emotional pain, you will feel it at times. It hurts, obviously, but just as there's no light without first the dark, there's no good without the bad. Pain is inevitable, so we just need to manage the bad when it comes.

Pain feels different to different people. I can't speak to your pain exactly, so I advise talking to someone who can. The way we deal with pain is also different. For me, I like opening up about it, just getting it off my chest, and sometimes that means in all caps, pressing very hard on my phone. Some people may need to rant to a friend or journal, exercise, or cry. There are unhealthy ways which you should try to avoid too, which would be like taking out anger which could damage people physiologically or physically.

Although we all deal with pain a little differently, the experience is common. It's okay to be down, to be sad. That's a normal side effect of pain, but at some point, you need to rise up, for your own sake, regardless of what is causing you pain.

The world can be a painful place, and life can hurt, but pain hurts twice as much if you let it stick with you. You may not be able to change what happened to you, but you can find your own healthy way to work toward healing the pain. You deserve happiness and comfort, so go find it. The best cure for pain is its opposite. You will heal by pursuing things like joy, because that is stronger than pain.

If you are in a home that brings a lot of hurt or pain and you can't control your environment – have hope that one day you will be 18 years old and can leave and make your life what you want it to be. Just hold on and focus on your future dreams of what you will make for yourself.

Pain can consume us if we let it. You can't stop the evil of this world, but you can make it better for yourself and those around you. Deal with your pain, and advocate for yourself and others. It's hard, and it is going to be a struggle. Don't fake anything-feeling the pain is a real emotion that can make you feel as if you're suffocating.

Pain thrives in lonely nights, sad movies, bitter songs, and tears. Feel the pain and let it out, but make the decision to not create more by feeding it. When you want to get rid of the pain, you may need to try different ways. Some may not work, but something will, so don't give up. Time can help you heal, and so can the commitment to address it. After the pain and the rain, the sun will rise, and with it, joy. Let that motivate you.

IGNORED

*Being ignored is a great privilege. That is how
I think I learned to see what others do not see
and to react to situations differently. I simply
looked at the world, not really prepared for
anything.*
—Saul Leiter

eing ignored sucks, whether it's not being heard, or being heard and
ignored, it all hurts. People can be mean, inconsiderate, and prejudiced--
they may fail to listen. Ignoring someone can impose silence in that person.
But silence may be one of the worst things for fighting evil, injustice, and
prejudice in this world. For when we are silent and scared, nothing gets done.
Silence is the fuel that feeds the fire of wrongdoing. In silence, no change is
brought about, no justice is alive, no one is heard. Too often, we accept being
ignored, for many reasons. We remain silent.

I wish it was as easy as simply being heard. Many of us teens and kids are
ignored for simply being at an age where we don't know anything. Apparently,
adults are the ones that know everything, and they should be the only ones heard.
Yet, is it not our generation who will be adults in a handful of years?

Being ignored can discourage us. This discouragement, in turn, causes us to
remain silent. You may be ignored by loads of people. I'm going to call anyone in
power or older than you or of a "higher ranking" an elder. Said elders may ignore
you. In fact, they almost certainly will at some point. Sometimes it is due to power
or ego, against which we must fight. Silence brings about no change. So, don't be
silent. Be annoying if you have to, but get your point across. Your ideas matter,
and you can change the world--no matter your age or position.

Imagine there is a young scientist in the world, and this scientist has been ignored all their life. They may have an idea that could cure every known disease, but because they have been ignored, they remain silent and let the other "elder" scientists promote their ideas instead.

You may be that scientist, a volcano waiting to erupt, and if that's you, erupt. Go change the world! If you're not being noticed, change what you're doing until you are. If people don't want to hear your idea, go off on your own to make your idea happen.

You should have seen the look on people's faces when I said I was writing a book. Now imagine if I would have listened, and gave up. Sometimes people need to be convinced to listen. So, if an anyone is ignoring you, don't be discouraged. Go out and be heard, in any way you can.

Elders aren't the only ones who may ignore you. Your peers can too, but give them a reason not to. Those who ignore you may do so because they think too highly of themselves, but on the inside, we are all the same. Or maybe they ignore you because they don't believe you or have faith in you. Prove them wrong. Create reasons to be heard, and be friends with people who respect you. They are out there.

Also, consider the possibility they aren't ignoring you at all, they just haven't yet had the opportunity to get to know you. Maybe you need to give them that opportunity.

Change only happens if you bring it about. Elders and peers may ignore you, but that doesn't matter. At some point, if you do enough, they will hear you. If you are passionate, if you want something bad enough, being ignored won't be an issue.

Whatever it is, don't stand for silence. So many issues in this world could have been, and still can be, solved by someone who will speak up and be heard. Think of any person who has brought about change in the world: Rosa Parks refused to give up her seat and started the boycott which would end segregation on the bus, Helen Keller who was blind & deaf but still learned to read and write and then advocated for those with disabilities, or Malala Yousufzai who didn't let an attempted assignation stop her from advocating for the right of women's education in Pakistan. They all made sure they were heard. All it takes is one person, one person to inspire others.

INCOMPETENT

*He attacked everything in life with a mix of
extraordinary genius and naive
incompetence, and it was often difficult to tell
which was which. —Douglas Adams*

You may have small insecurities about different parts of yourself, but when those insecurities add up, they create a feeling of incompetence. It is very easy for anyone to feel this way, and much depends on what you do to feel like you're enough.

If you're reading this, you are likely putting effort into an area that doesn't complete you. There are so many temptations in the world of things we are supposed to do to feel good about ourselves. To me, most of these efforts to feel good don't work and won't work. They are impossible, flawed, or have too many loopholes. If you allow one these flawed things to be the foundation upon which your self-image lies, your house will not be very sturdy. Any person will be able to knock you down.

I get how easy it is to feel as if you're not good enough, but some things are designed so that you will never feel good enough. Even if you do exactly what you have been hoping to do, it will still never be enough. You may want to be super rich and famous and think when you are it will be enough. After some time, you can be rich and it still may not be enough, because there is always going to be someone with more money.

So, ask yourself: what are you doing to try to feel like you're enough? If you are trying to please everyone, it's impossible. Trying to be cool enough by other's opinions or striving to be popular are flawed attempts at wholeness. Having others tell you that you are good enough sounds nice, but it doesn't change who you are.

There are endless ways we try to feel complete, and so many of them set you up to fail. To me, there is only one way to truly feel complete-it starts in your heart.

Your heart is stronger than your mind, so if you feel complete in your heart, your mind will follow. There are different ways to feel complete, such as helping others, spreading happiness, and maintaining a positive attitude, but these approaches can waiver in hard times.

No matter what happens, focus on being yourself. That is the strongest foundation you can lay. Don't let others label you. Be yourself and love yourself. You cannot please others, or ever feel cool enough, or be fulfilled by their opinions. What you can do is please yourself, be yourself, and fulfill yourself.

You'll never be perfect, and when we try to be, that is when we feel incompetent. When we try to do things that are impossible, we fail, and in that failure lies the feeling of incompetence. Instead of trying for impossible standards, when we just learn to accept and embrace ourselves on the inside and, no one will ever knock us down.

The strongest security for feeling like you're not good enough is realizing you already are good enough. Who even creates these standards of beauty and strength and looks and smarts? People who want you to buy products to help "improve" these qualities in yourself.

I challenge you to create your own standards. Set them for who YOU want to become. When you reach them, you will feel as if you are good enough. It may not be easy if you are used to putting all this effort into being good enough for others, but here is the thing: you will never _feel_ good enough until you stop trying to be good enough and _realize_ you already are.

INSECURE

Everybody has something they hate about themselves. Some of us can think of hundreds of things, and some may just have one. Things we cannot change, but will spend time and money trying to. Things that make us unique, but when we look in the mirror, we do not see unique. We see wrong.

This isn't abnormal or surprising, because society has mistakenly labeled "different" as wrong. If we do not have the exact ideal female model body, then we are ugly. If we do not get 100 percent on our math test, then we are not smart. If we do not have a cute laugh, then we sound stupid when we laugh. There are many things to be insecure about. On the other hand, there is absolutely nothing to be insecure about because those things make up who you are.

You may not be the perfect model, the best at math, or have a cute laugh, but none of those things make you bad. They make you, you! And you are amazing! Each person is truly unique from everyone else. We often promote diversity in society, but we forget to tell people as individuals how amazing they are. The best things to do if you feel insecure are to admit it and embrace it.

Surprisingly, we don't often admit our insecurities to ourselves, let alone other people. But it's very good to admit what you don't like about yourself. It can be hard to admit our insecurities, because we often have them for no reason. You hate that you don't look a certain way or don't have a certain skill, but it isn't anyone's fault--it's just the way life is.

But life is also who you should be thanking because you have gifts that others don't have. That's the great thing about our differences, not any of us are the same, thank goodness!

We all have things we are insecure about, and once we admit and realize them, we can begin to flip the way we think about them. Maybe we don't feel the prettiest or we have a mole, but it's who we are. Embrace those things. Don't let someone else's comment get you down. Wear your insecurities like they're gold, and embrace them--and soon they won't be insecurities. Soon, when someone makes a remark it won't affect you. Your negative self-talk will go away, and your self-confidence will grow.

Admit and embrace. Admit and embrace. Admit and embrace.

IRRELEVANT

Experience has shown, and a true philosophy
will always show, that a vast, perhaps the
larger portion of the truth arises from the
seemingly irrelevant.
—Edgar Allan Poe

rrelevant is a word we may often call a famous person, or some random YouTuber. Maybe even other people. But for yourself, it's more of an issue. You may feel like when people invite you places, you're just kind of there. Everybody has a best friend and all these people they connect with, and you're there too-but not where you want to be. You may feel that people don't like you or care about you. It's a completely reasonable feeling, and it may or may not be true.

You can have hundreds of friends and still feel completely irrelevant because, to feel significant you need more than just simple friendships-you need deep connections with people, and a relatively positive self-image.

Believing that you are not relevant hurts the way you think about yourself. I challenge you to stop people-pleasing and doing things to try to make other people like you. So often we change our character for others. It may sound normal, but it is terrible. You cannot feel relevant if you aren't yourself. You won't feel complete or that you are enough. It may seem like happiness, but true happiness comes from being yourself.

When you are yourself people will like you -maybe not everyone, but those who matter will. Your friends are your friends, and they care about you. Connect with new people, and be yourself. That alone should make you feel relevant. You may never feel the most popular or smartest or anything else. That is okay, because you don't need to be any of those things.

You need to be yourself. If you feel like no one understands you right now in your life, ask yourself this: are you letting fear determine that? Are you afraid for people to see the real you? If so, put down any tough act you've been using and be yourself. You will find people who treat you like the king or queen you are. You will find true happiness in expressing your emotions.

Your relevance comes from within. If you try to gain that from others, it won't work. So, stop trying. Be yourself and people will like you. Your life isn't meant for you to be someone else. You will be you, and your relevance and significance will soar from that.

You don't have to go through life pleasing others. If you are not found yet, you will be soon. Through being yourself, you will become satisfied with your life. People will connect with you on real levels, and soon all this popularity rigamarole won't matter.

If you feel like no one is paying attention to you or would care if you went away, you're wrong. Just wait. It may take a while, but eventually the people in your life will come around. I know how it feels, but the wait is worth finally feeling noticed again.

It doesn't matter how many friends or followers you have. What matters is this: when things get tough, how many people are you able to talk to? That is the number of real friends you have. Put your time into those relationships and not into improving the general population's opinion of you. Through this, you will feel relevant to someone, and that is worth more than anything.

IRRITATED

I don't have pet peeves, I have whole kennels
of irritation.
—Whoopi Goldberg

A nyone can get riled up and lash out. Irritation is a big cause of this. Irritated and annoyed are similar feelings, but irritation is a stronger, deeper emotion that can shorten our patience to the point where we are just kind of done and angry.

When you're irritated, it is no fun for you or the people around you. Some days you are irritated more easily and on others you can withstand the temptations. So many things can irritate us for so many reasons--and sometimes for no reason at all. You just have to learn to stay true to yourself. You can't always stop the source of your irritation. You can stop your negative reaction though.

I don't know why humans are wired to get angry and negatively react sometimes. Maybe we used this emotion as a defense mechanism. Maybe it is a side effect of our complex relationships and emotions. I'm not sure. I do believe that it causes a lot of destruction.

If you have never lashed out at someone and then immediately asked yourself why you just said that, good job-but you probably will respond this way at some point. Irritation may not cause this strong of a reaction in you, but it sure can cause some kind of reaction. If someone or something is irritating you and you can make an effort to stop it, then do so. Lots of instances in life aren't that cut and dried. So, if you can't stop someone or something else, you must control yourself instead.

All it takes is self-control. This is a hard thing to learn for many, yet in life you must make an effort to. Think of something that could put pressure on someone, like not performing well in class. In this kind of situation, you can imagine someone who gets very angry and blames others, and then you can imagine someone who keeps their cool and learns from the situation. Lack of self-control vs. self-control.

Irritation can arise from a variety of similar circumstances. You will feel irritated at different times in your life, I guarantee it. Something, sometime, is going to make you mad. It's a natural thing. The important thing is that you don't let it affect you negatively.

Don't let irritation get into your heart. Find the calm in the storm. Is whatever is irritating you worth more than a calm mood? If it isn't, don't work against yourself. It may not be easy, but you can keep calm in any irritating situation if you care enough. Realize you are wound up and take a second to draw a few deep breaths, to calm down. I don't think lashing out has ever been the best decision, but if you let irritation control you, it is the only decision you will ever make.

We've talked about what to do to control yourself, but let me make another thing clear: irritation can be a good thing too. If you're irritated about something like injustice, that is great. We should challenge the wrong we see in the world, and if you are personally angry about something, it helps bring change. Use those feelings as motivation, but not as an internal dictatorship. One of the pros of experiencing irritation is that we now know what needs to change around us.

Consider all the people who have brought about change in the world. These people let their voices be heard, but they did it in smart ways. There are healthy and positive methods for expressing your irritation, frustration, and anger, and the best approaches will bring about change in new ways.

ISOLATED

If isolation temper the strong, it is the
stumbling-block of the uncertain.
—*Paul Cezanne*

The feeling of isolation is a combination of feeling different and being alone. When you are isolated, you still know people are there . . . it is just a question of who is really there when times get tough. Who really values your friendship, and who is just there because they kind of like you?

When you go through isolation, you feel different and left out of everything, as if you are the odd one out. No one is on the same page as you, and although you are physically in sync with your friends, mentally and emotionally you are miles apart. It doesn't matter if you feel isolated when you are by yourself at 3:00 a.m. or when you are at the busiest place in the world--true isolation leaves you feeling completely alone.

Isolation usually isn't something you do to yourself; it is a feeling. A feeling of where you are in comparison to everyone else, and specifically, that you are not the same as everyone else. It's a very hard realization, since most people are obsessed with fitting in, because that is the goal of life, right? Wrong.

If isolation is a feeling, how do we prevent it? First, consider that you may be just like your friends, and this could be all in your head. Of course, it is in your head, because it's an emotion, but you could be overthinking it. People are way more alike than you would believe, and a little difference is actually good for a friendship or friend group. When negative thoughts rise in a positive environment, step out of your mind for a moment, and look around with your eyes.

I cannot guarantee that you will be exactly like your friends--you may never have that "thing" you connect over, or that one inside joke, or half the same problems--but you have each other. The best friendships don't require two identical people--they can be opposites, or not opposites, or whatever. Don't overcomplicate it. You may be different from your friends, but you call them friends for a reason. Try not to isolate yourself into this feeling, because being different is great. Embrace your own uniqueness, but realize you are not alone. You are not the weird one in the group; you are the only you in the group. If people don't value you and appreciate the unique you, find some new friends. Stay strong, and derive strength from the way you are.

The loneliness that comes from being different is what makes us feel isolated. The same facts that would be meant to affirm this feeling can actually reverse it. You are different than every single person. That doesn't mean you're alone. It means we are all alone. If we are all alone, then no one is. In our isolation, we are all together.

If you are truly feeling isolated, reach out to people, get active and find things to do that bring joy. Often it takes taking a break from social media and having direct interactions to feel more in touch with people and less isolated, so try reaching out to friends and connecting face to face.

JEALOUS

I'm kind of jealous of the life I'm supposedly leading. —Zach Braff

Jealousy is a word we hear about others and see as a negative trait. Though it is a negative trait, it is one we all have and will feel in our lifetime. Often, it is controllable-we are jealous, but some people are lucky. Some people were born with the blessings we want, as we take our own for granted. A hard lesson to learn is it's okay to compare your life to others, but not to hate your own and don't make that your standard for success.

We so often see things, especially in today's online culture, that make us jealous. We must try and halt this feeling, because it brings only bitterness, resentment, and discontent. We find ourselves drawn to hatred of others, or hatred of life's luck-or lack of it.

You're not wrong for feeling jealous--you're never wrong for <u>feeling</u> anything. What can be wrong is what we do with those feelings. We must appreciate this emotion, but also try to turn it into something that can benefit us, and our vision on life.

A hard truth to accept is that there is a very small chance you will be the best in the world at something. You can do it with hard work and determination, but it's hard to be the best in a world of talented people. So, why do we feel bad if we're not the best at something, or perhaps anything? It's because we have a natural compulsion to compare, which leads to jealousy. Online, nearly everything is edited and not necessarily realistic. Real life . . . is rarely like what you see online. Even so, try to feel happy for those "lucky" people. You'll find much more happiness and contentment in your heart by giving someone credit when they do something good or celebrating with them when they receive something good, instead of wishing it was you. When you do this, jealousy fades.

Some may not often feel jealous, but can still wish to be smarter, prettier, or richer. If you truly can work for it and you want to, what is stopping you? This isn't the true problem though. The problem is that we can always find things to complain about and things always appear better when viewed from afar.

Many people on this planet are at a loss for food, clean water, good health, basic human rights, shelter, safety, a voice, and freedom. Many of us reading this book have all of these things. We often overlook the little things and take them for granted, yet others are very jealous of us just having basic needs. In fact, if you live in the USA like me, you are wealthy – the poorest people living in the USA are wealthier than 70% of the rest of the world.

When you start to realize maybe you won't be the richest ever, but you have a roof over your head and food on your plate, you find your happy. Life will be life; try your best to pursue happiness, but you must also appreciate the happiness that is already around you. Stop taking things for granted, and value the invaluable. When you do, in your mind, you will be the richest and luckiest person in this world.

Jealousy is common--it is everywhere. It fuels feelings of hate, and hatred fuels many of the things that are wrong in the world. When we learn to make lemonade out of the lemons that life gives us, we feel refreshed and content-even when things don't turn out the way we would have liked. We begin to see everything that is great, and we can spend our time on self-improvement and doing fun things, instead of sitting in sorrow. If you look for the positive, you will find it.

Jealousy will still pop up, and when it does, feel no shame. Accept it as an opportunity to reflect on the greatness, of yourself, of your gifts, of your privileges. When we start to build each other up and love what we have, we all go further, together.

(LIKE JUST A) KID

*I think, for many teens, a fundamental fact of
the teenage experience is that you're in
between this childlike state, in which you're
told you're completely unqualified for just
about anything in the adult world, and this
adult world, where you're being told you have
to be responsible, and you're just trying to
figure out where you stand.*
—Cole Sprouse

The current age has brought the means for freedom and happiness for kids. Sure enough, we prepare for life by going to school and doing well within our own studies and subjects. Most of us aren't forced into factories to work all day, a thing we should all be very thankful for.

Be thankful for the things you are provided with, because around the world kids do not have these luxuries. With youth and age restrictions come the feeling of not being as important or capable as adults, like we can't do something. While I would not suggest trying to drive if you're underage, or do anything else that breaks the law, it's important to recognize that being a kid is an opportunity, not a limit.

As kids, we have youth-we have time and, most importantly, we have the element of surprise. Many adults don't expect us to do great things; they expect quite the opposite, really. Being young, we have time on our hands. Do your schoolwork first, and meet all your commitments too. But you have time to spare, which you can use for having fun or doing something important.

If you're reading this, it's because you want to do something, but you feel limited by a number that determines how many 365-day cycles have gone by since you came into the world. Don't let this stop you from anything.

If you want to do something, you can. You have time and youth on your side. Many people genuinely think kids can't do great things because we are too young or too inexperienced. Sometimes, we start to believe this. The idea of doing great things is something we save for when we are older. Yet, this isn't true.

Right now, I'm fourteen, and I have time and youth, so I use it. I could come up with ideas and let them pass by. I could have a mindset where kids don't do amazing things, but that would be a limited mindset. Now I'm not saying I'm perfect, but I am a kid. If you see this as a disadvantage, you are playing the wrong game, because being a kid can be amazing.

Many people would probably think I know nothing about emotions or how to help people. We need leaders, and you are not just a kid. You are a person, so go out there and prove those people wrong. When you do something great, it will be that much better. Have fun too, but if you want to change this world, you can.

Being a kid, you may feel disrespected or unheard--I've been there. Don't do anything illegal or unsafe, but if you want to make a positive impact now, why would you ever wait until you're one of those people (an adult) who stopped you? One day you will have your time to shine; for now, do your best and don't let anyone stop you from chasing your dreams because you're too young.

LACKING

Be content with what you have; rejoice in the way things are. When you realize there is nothing lacking, the whole world belongs to you. —Lao Tzu

I n our daily routine, we manage to see a lack perfection in just about every single way. That's the thing-we compare ourselves, and everything about ourselves, to others. Of course, you're not the very best at everything. Maybe you even feel like you're not the very best at anything. Trust me, you don't need to be.

We often feel lacking because we see others who we think aren't. We see the most beautiful people online or in a magazine and think, *why am I not this pretty? I lack in the area of being beautiful.* You try really hard and study for a test. Yet, all your friends still score better. By comparing yourself to others, you irreversibly set yourself up for failure. So, don't compare; instead, appreciate.

Look at yourself in the mirror and tell yourself you're beautiful. What even is beautiful? This is a word we all define differently, but I promise someone out there will think you are the most beautiful person in the world. You are not a failure or lacking in smarts because you got an F on a test or assignment. Just study harder next time, and identify what you did wrong so you can improve. Maybe you aren't the best at social situations and struggle to make new friends. Then push yourself to go out there and make new friends. Be yourself.

Everyone has potential to do great things. I wrote this book based on that belief. You can do great things, and no part of you is wrong. No part of you needs to be changed or is lacking. You are you. Embrace that and accept it, and don't change for others.

Go out there and do something great. Push yourself every day. Some of us may still feel lacking, even at our highest of highs. But as we look down the mountain we just summited, we mustn't forget where we came from and compare that to where we are now.

LAME

*I got joked on. You had people saying I was
stupid, that I was lame, that I was feminine,
this and that. I was like, 'OK, but I'm still
gonna be successful, and you're not.'*
—Khalid

L ame can be a somewhat "fun" word. Maybe not so fun if you feel like you're
lame, but a fun word regardless. You see, I say this because I believe no one
is lame. Everyone is them, and if being "boring" is what you like doing, then
do it. Too many of us feel that lameness has negative effects, as if people think
they are uncool or a wimp. Why would people ever want someone like that as a
friend? Sure, people like fun and go-getters, but people also just like people. When
it comes down to it, don't change who you are . . . but it's good to push yourself
outside of your comfort zone.

This whole idea of being lame goes hand in hand with peer pressure. Trust me,
what you believe in is greater than the opinions of others, and even if you always
give in, it won't fill your heart. Being "cool" isn't the solution for feeling lame.

Now, that is contradictory to everything you have probably heard: lame and
cool are like opposites, so if you are lame you must try to strive for being cool. This
isn't true. We feel lame because of others. If there was no one around, you couldn't
apply a "cool factor," so you would never feel lame. The fact that someone out
there is unhappy with themselves because they are not cool enough or popular
enough is one of society's biggest flaws.

If you try your whole life to be cool or popular or whatever, it will never be
enough. You will not find true happiness in that pursuit. So, if you believe you are
lame, then change your view of the word.

Don't beat yourself up for not fitting the perfect standards of being good enough or cool enough. If you do, you will never stop beating yourself up. You might be lame according to those standards, and the fact you feel that way is sad to me. It is not your fault for feeling this way, but I wish to save you this sadness.

If you truly believe you are lame, I get it. It is so easy to feel this way in the current age. So, go find some lame friends to hang with. What I mean is, find some friends based on the people they are. Make friendships with people based on how they treat you and whether they care about you. Nothing else. Not popularity, not rumors . . . nothing but relational experience. If you try to be cool and do all these things, you will still live your whole life thinking you are lame. There will always be the new cool thing, and you may not agree with it. Instead, embrace who you are. Embrace your lack of coolness.

I dream of a world where people don't worry about being popular or cool, where instead they worry about their five best friends and because they do, they help each other. I know it may seem like just a dream, but it doesn't have to be. All it takes is one inspirational person at your school, who lives their life.

Be that person. Don't worry about others or this made-up social status. Worry about the ones you love. When you do that, you may still be the lamest person in the world, according to the "cool" people, but you won't care, because there is a security in true friendship, and none in popularity.

LONELY

If I'm a legend, then why am I so lonely? —
Judy Garland

It's a Saturday night, and you were forced to stay home for whatever reason. Now you're alone while all your friends are hanging out. Naturally, you feel lonely and left out. Loneliness is being single while all your friends are not. Loneliness is when you're in that room of people but have no one to talk to.

You may have five hundred friends or five friends, it doesn't matter. What matters is when you are going through a hard time, who can cheer you up? Who will drop everything for you, because they care about you? The answer is real friends-best friends. Hold on to these people and never let them go, and if they help you, help them. You always need the person you can call at 3:00 a.m. and know they will answer.

Some of us struggle. We may have these friends, but we've been brainwashed into believing they don't care. If someone asks you to help, say yes. You want to be happy; you don't want to bring someone down too. If someone offers you help, receive it graciously. You know if your best friends care about you, and if you think they do, they do.

The most important thing to do when you're lonely, is not turn on sad music, which will only make you feel lonelier. It's important to express your feelings, but connect with people, rather than wallowing alone. Maybe try reaching out to someone you have not connected to in a while. One of the best ways to become happy is to spread it.

If you truly are lonely, it may be hard to feel like you want to be liberated. We can get used to being alone all the time. Even in our minds, we may feel alone all the time.

It is human nature to connect with others and find good healthy relationships. Those people are out there, I swear. Sometimes you just have to keep looking.

LOST

We're not lost. We're locationally challenged.
—John M. Ford

ost is possibly the most cliché "developing teenager" feeling ever. Also, perhaps the most real. In life, so much goes on it's easy to feel disconnected at any point. At this age, we can get caught up in sports, hobbies, and even on stuff like social media. It's no surprise we can feel lost.

You see a post of your best friends hanging out without you. It hurts, and you begin to question them, but then you also begin to question yourself. *Why am I not good enough?* This spiral goes down a few more chains, and suddenly we feel like a plastic bag drifting through the wind. Lost.

When we feel lost, we just need to find our way back. The easiest way to do so is to calm down and put your emotions on hold. Reconcile your options and address the situation. We can learn a lot from self-reflection, if we let ourselves. I promise you, there are good people in the world, a good place for you. If you haven't found it, it doesn't mean you're lost. But rather, traveling, down the path of destiny.

Just remember, if you feel lost, it's often a misunderstanding, a common occurrence in our world. Remember this too: nobody gets out of a maze by giving up.

MISPLACED

Celebrate the idea that you don't fit in. Find your own fit. Stay unique.
—Betsey Johnson

The world wants you to be perfect. And no one is. We often feel like we're not in the right place, and it's not someone else's fault--it is ours. We often get so caught up in the negative aspects of our life, we fail to see that we are in the right place.

Many of us look around and feel we don't fit in. Like nobody cares, nobody wants us. Sometimes it feels as if everybody hates us-even people we don't know. It's a real fear and a real reality. We can't make new friends and we struggle in social situations. It's tough. Often, it seems so bad that we decide to give up and be self-reliant, alone all the time. At the time, it seems reasonable, but it slowly leads to more sadness. All from the misperception of the way people think of us.

Most of the time, our perception isn't true. We need to first start talking positive inside. Put yourself out there and try to make new friends. Even if it doesn't work, you lose nothing. I promise you, wherever you are there is someone who will love every bit of you. For who you are and no other reason. All it takes is one nice person to change the way you think and make you believe in the good of society. If you let the fear of denial stop you from getting out there, you won't find your way out of the place you are in. You must have some sacrifice.

It sounds simple, but I understand it's not always that simple. You have to put in some effort. You will find your people, and maybe it's not who you would except. Maybe you feel you don't need other people, but we all do. We find more in relationships with others than in anything else.

If you ever feel misplaced, you need to gain trust in this system we call life. If you feel misplaced, find yourself in other people. I know it seems crazy, but out there somewhere are your best friends, and just because you haven't met the right people yet-or your right people aren't really the right people-doesn't mean they aren't out there. Everyone has someone, including you. Now go out there and find them.

MISUNDERSTOOD

To be great is to be misunderstood.
—Ralph Waldo Emerson

We all experience a wide range of emotions. People really aren't that different from each other. In this world, however, we often don't feel this way. We feel as if nobody is like us, nobody understands us, and nobody is ever going to understand us. I get it. We often feel bad for ourselves, hide our emotions, and lock them inside. We get so caught up in believing other things that we begin to mentally break the bonds that connect us with society. Sometimes this isn't a terrible thing, but we usually feel misunderstood when we're not connected.

Nobody understands me. If you have never said this to yourself, then you have heard it. When we are sad or angry or feeling some other emotion, sometimes all we want is someone to relate to us. To feel as if maybe you are not going through this alone. Maybe you are not the only one out there who is struggling. We often can't find this person. Everybody we turn to either doesn't care or doesn't understand. This leads to frustration, and we begin to not even try to express ourselves to others. We may have a hundred friends or just one, but we live in fear of embarrassment and are too afraid to say how we really feel. We feel like nobody understands because, thus far, no one has.

I too have often felt this way. I had begun to come to terms with the fact that I was different. Until out of the blue someone said something that made me realize we were very alike. I wasn't convinced, initially, but I heard them out. I realized I wasn't that weird. I was a little disappointed at first, but still amazed that someone actually understood me.

You too, will find someone who is like you, and someone who you can tell all your problems to, who understands and cares about you. I can't say when, because

I do not know. But don't lose hope. We are all in it together, and we can help each other.

You are not misunderstood. You may be unlucky, but everyone is different and there is absolutely nothing wrong with you or the way you are. You are unique, but someone will understand you. Whatever you're going through, someone else has been through it or is going through it right now.

Never be afraid to talk about the way you feel, because there is nothing wrong with how you feel. You are not alone, and when you feel like no one else cares, know that I do-even if we haven't met.

NUMB

I learned to be with myself rather than
avoiding myself with limiting habits; I started
to be aware of my feelings more, rather than
numb them.
—Judith Wright

Numb ... the feeling of no feeling. The feeling that you can feel more strongly than any other emotion. Pain is something we learn to get used to. Don't believe me? Think of hot water in the shower. How long does it really stay hot? Until we get used to it. We can turn the water up, up, and up, but each time we do, we feel no burning heat just a short while later.

Similarly, the pain in our hearts will slowly increase until we can't feel it anymore. You would think this is a good thing, but feeling nothing is worse. You're already used to the pain, so when you feel nothing, deep down, the pain is still there. Deep down, where it hurts, you feel every single bit of that pain. On the outside you may be silent, but the inside screams like nails on a chalkboard.

Feeling numb is complicated. Back to my example with hot water, even if you don't feel the pain of the burning anymore, you still have to turn off the shower or it can seriously hurt you.

Emotions are the one way humans have survived, the one way people are unique. We are not the fastest, strongest, biggest, or really the best at anything, but we have a brain capable of thinking and feeling an array of emotions. So, when we feel absolutely nothing, we lose a big part of what makes us human and special.

I know that sometimes you get tired of the pain, the crying, the hopelessness, the isolation. It makes total sense. Those things are terrible, the worst in the world. I know it adds up, and you come to a certain point where it feels like it all goes away. It may seem like the best option, the most bearable option. But one thing to understand is that your emotions - the pain, the crying, the hopelessness – big, flashing signs that something needs to change. Embracing numbness is ignoring the signs you are sending to yourself.

In life, we can't always just turn off the hot water. It may even be a struggle to cool the water down a little. In those times, brave the pain. Fight the numbness, because when you are numb, all the bad stuff goes straight to your soul and eats you away. That is real damage-the feeling could make you lose who you are.

For some of us, this may seem better than the pain, but it isn't. You must fight the pain, and you fight it by feeling it. Feel the pain. I know it hurts, but you must keep yourself. Feel the pain and you feel the happiness. When you feel numb, you feel neither.

It will be tough, but feeling numb isn't good for you. You may prevent the bad, but you also miss out on the good. Even if there may be no good in your life right now, it won't always be. It will get better. Understand what is pushing you over and address it. Too often we feel the pain we know, but we don't know the pain we feel.

Feeling numb ... it's tough. It's a lot of questioning. *What should I do?* Too often we decide to do nothing. But we need to fight this pain. Even if you think you have nothing to fight for, you fight for the fact you will if you keep going. Feeling nothing hurts what makes us, us. That very thing is the single most important part of who you are-it is you.

Sometimes feeling this requires serious help. If you think that's you, find someone to whom you can describe what you feel, even if it is nothing. Numbness may literally seem and feel like nothing, but remember that without bad there is no good.

OVERLOOKED

*I would rather write or record something
great and have it overlooked than do
mediocre work and have it be popular.*
—Patti Smith

I t's very hard to keep pushing, thriving, or doing amazing things when you receive almost no immediate praise, reward or even acknowledgement. It's even harder when you're doing those things to the best of your ability and confidence but someone else is getting credit, recognition, or rewards. This kind of experience is a test of our character, to keep pushing even when we're not getting what we want or what we think we deserve. If you pass this test, it will be a first step to achieving greater things and being happier than before.

Whatever you're doing – work, school, sports, chores – do the best you can, all the time. Many already do this all the time. In fact, right now we may have everything going for us . . . we are doing great, better than ever before, yet we aren't getting the satisfaction. We feel unlucky or unappreciated, and it doesn't add up. The good karma in life isn't there, or isn't giving back to us. All the hard work is for what seems like nothing.

It's natural to want something in return, and want it now. A tough lesson is that you're not always going to get that. An opportunity will come, one that you will take, and you will reap the rewards. One day your hard work will pay off. You will not be overlooked, but looked at over everyone else. Have patience, and don't give up if it hasn't happened yet. Life is a journey, and you may miss out on one thing that ends up making room for something even better.

But let's say the opportunity isn't coming. Every day you do your best-no rewards, no promotion-you're just there, waiting for the opportunity of your lifetime. It may come, or it may not.

So, go make the opportunity of your lifetime. If you are confident in what you do, show it. Advocate for yourself, because though sometimes other might advocate for you, why depend on others for your success?

Don't sit back and let your voice be unheard. That's not how we improve-that's how we stay exactly the same. If you're happy doing the same thing and never going above and beyond, then fine, embrace that choice and value the decision you've made. But if you want to go and do amazing things, then understand that you it may take commitment and long effort. Just because others overlook you, don't let that be an excuse to overlook yourself.

I have confidence that everyone reading this book will get many opportunities, lucky or unlucky. Be ready, look for it, and opportunity will come. You can change the world. Remain true to yourself through time of hardship and no reward. When the opportunity comes, be you, take it, and it you will see the reward.

OVERWHELMED

Many of us feel stress and get overwhelmed
not because we're taking on too much,
but because we're taking on too little of
what really strengthens us.
—Marcus Buckingham

Today, like every day, you probably did hundreds of things. For each task you are expected to reach certain standards, spend a certain amount of time, or achieve a minimum score. All these things in one day, or even a week, begin to add up. Like a Thanksgiving meal, there is too much on our plate. These responsibilities - schoolwork, commitments, plans - seem impossible to get done, while still get a reasonable amount of sleep. (And sometimes we do have to sacrifice some sleep to get things done!) The feeling of being overwhelmed can drive us crazy and build up a tension that needs to be eased.

In your life – and most likely in the next week – there will be times you feel overwhelmed. There will be a million things to get done and about an hour of time.

First things first, make sure you're managing your time. If you know you have a homework project due and sports practice, then don't waste two hours on your phone. Plan ahead and manage your time. This will prevent you from being overwhelmed as often. Put your priorities and commitments first, and when they are finished, any side projects or fun activities can follow. If you are not good at managing your time, admit but work on it. Plan it out, write it down, hold yourself accountable – or ask someone else to. The more you begin to be organized, the less overwhelmed you will feel.

On the other hand, being overwhelmed isn't something you can always prepare for. Teachers, parents, coaches, bosses – they all sometimes throw things on you at one time. It can be frustrating, but try to blame them. Instead, use these feelings of annoyance and frustration as motivation to get your work done. You may feel stressed and tense, so try a 5 or 10 minute break and spend some time on yourself. You need to relieve this stress, so go for a walk or do something that will take you away from your stress – just don't lose track of time!

Once you have settled down, you have stuff to do. Before you start working, plan ahead and prioritize. Work on the important things first. You may not finish everything, and that's okay. Make sure you are focused on the task at hand, instead of worrying about all the tasks you have to do. Don't get on your phone or take a break every 5 minutes, instead reward yourself with short breaks after completing a task. Work hard and smart, and you will finish by taking one step at a time. You may have to sacrifice some personal time, or sleep, but you will finish. Do everything with quality and without rushing, so you won't have to do a redo.

In life, you will feel overwhelmed. It's challenging to get stuff done in a time filled with school, homework, sports, family commitments and so much more. Life doesn't always get less stressful, but if you take it step by step, you can learn to manage it. I can't say you'll enjoy it. You may be continue to feel frustrated, and let out a few too many sighs along the way, but that's normal. Know what you are doing, go do your work, and strive to do your best. I know you can do it. Use your emotions to motivate yourself. When you are done, you'll feel pride in your work.

Finally, make sure you prioritize getting enough rest and sleep. Our body recovers during sleep and it repairs our physical and mental health. When we get less than we need, then we tend to get overwhelmed more easily because we are tired. Take care of your body to reduce physical and mental distress.

PARANOID

I guess the line between being paranoid
and being a rock star is smaller than
one would expect.
—Brian Molko

There's no doubt we often overthink things. And when we do, it's usually not the best idea. Thoughts come to mind that are not even true or relevant, but they still affect us. Overthinking something you are scared about is an example of being paranoid. We get lost in our minds, in the false ideas, in our biggest fears. It changes the way we think and our actions. It increases our fears, and we become worried about the little things.

Everything is scary, until it isn't. Some of us feel this way in situations all the time, for reasons that range from absolutely no reason to issues from our past. Ironically, the best way to fix this is to think--just a lot less.

Feelings of paranoia just build and build if we don't stop it. This isn't good-- it's scary, and it causes us to be weird. Weird in a way of being sensitive and afraid.

At some point when you are paranoid, you have a moment where you notice it. When you do, it's good to acknowledge that you might be having irrational fears. Calm down, if possible. We all have our own ways of doing this. Think about the things that bring you calm and peace, and do those things when you begin to feel paranoid.

We sometimes begin to think irrationally, so try to reverse this and bring yourself down to Earth. Whatever is freaking you out, be realistic about it. Try to think the situation over logically and feed the logical thoughts and not the irrational thoughts. You can make that choice. The more we do this in times of stress, the easier it will become.

It's also good to talk about your feelings or write down what you're thinking. Releasing the thoughts aloud helps you calm down and really hear or see what you're thinking. Once you're calm, begin to think about what is causing you to be paranoid. Most of the time it's a fear - acknowledge and admit it to yourself. Then try to figure out why you're afraid.

Let's say you have a fear of haunted houses. The reason why is that you don't want to be tortured or murdered, and that seems like something that might occur at a haunted house. Sometimes identifying the fear - and the reason for it - isn't this easy. We may fear something more serious but also not want to face it. Or our past may be fueling a fire bigger than we know how to handle. Fear is natural, but we want to make sure we don't let it control us.

Paranoia in any case is scary, stressful, and uncomfortable. Talk it out with a friend, and if it's something serious - not a small, fixable issue - please seek professional help. Many of us have things we are so afraid of and sometimes we need some help.

Your fears are just an obstacle that you can and will overcome. Realize you're being irrational and do something about it. You're never wrong for feeling this way. We all freak out sometimes, but remember that you don't have to face it alone. Life is seeded in happiness and positivity - you just have to plant it.

PRESSURED

Pressure is an emotional paralysis. It's hard
enough to do the dishes when you're feeling
pressured, let alone make a movie.
—Jennifer Lynch

Our modern, online world demands a lot of us. It can feel like there is always a crowd watching us and one mistake can mess everything up and set your whole life on a different path. The feeling of people counting on you combined with self-doubt can be very intense. Pressure comes from all sorts of places: parents, teachers, teammates, coaches, ourselves, you name it. It really adds up and makes us feel like everything in life is a test - one we are going to fail. Pressures create added stress, shortens our temper, and can make life less enjoyable. The pressure is there, and it can get in our head.

A big part of the pressure you feel may be the doubt you have about yourself, or the fear of failure. You wouldn't feel pressure if you knew that ten out of ten times you would succeed. You care about the people who look over you, and do not want to let them down. But maybe there is a different way to look at things, for in life, we get many chances.

If you truly give it your all and things still don't go your way, you may be disappointed, but in reality, you didn't fail anyone. You probably learned a lesson a grew a bit. If you didn't give it your all, that's okay too - learn from that and consider what you want to do differently next time. You will get another opportunity. Take your lumps, think about it, talk with friends, regroup, and then go try again - that's all you can do.

For many of us, pressure can get in the way of doing our best. I understand what it's like to have people you don't want to let down. The insane amount of pressure messes with us. Instead of focusing on the task at hand, we begin to overthink and worry. We drift away from what we are doing and lose focus.

In times of pressure, try to acknowledge it and take a few minutes to calm yourself in a healthy way. Take deep breaths, and do what you need to do to focus. Rejuvenate and refocus. Don't worry about other people, other things that need to be done, or the outcome. Work hard, and try your best now, focusing on the task at hand.

Remember, pressure is relative. No matter where you are in your life, certain task will feel urgent and important - like they may change your life. But most things won't completely affect your life in a negative way if you mess up. Don't overthink it, and have confidence in your ability. When the pressure builds up, reconnect with yourself. Find yourself in this time of pressure, for only you can do it. Try your best and if you've done so, be proud.

REGRETFUL

I can remember watching 'Lord of the Rings'
and being truly regretful that I
wasn't a being in that world.
—Chris Hemsworth

The past has such an impact on us. We often linger over it, and in the worst way. We forgot the good, remember the bad, and let our own mistakes shine above all else. We look back and we don't forgive or move on. We look back at all the things we regret doing and ask why? Why did I ever do this? At the time, there was probably a reason, and at that time it seemed like a good one. Now, however, we look back and see the effects of our decision and we regret what we did.

The past is called the past for a reason. It's behind us. The events have passed us by and are now history. Many of us hate history class, but still feel attached to our very own history.

Look, no one is perfect. No one has ever gone through life and made the correct decision every single time. We all mess up, and that's okay. What's not okay is letting those mistakes define who we are.

Now, you may look back and hate what you did, but the simple fact is, you did it. There's nothing you can do now to change that. Don't let that be the reason you regret it. Instead, let it be the reason you move on.

The thing you regret is probably something you messed up on. If you let that one mistake be all you think about, it can overshadow your life.

We look at the past to learn for the future. So, think back on whatever you regret right now. You messed up, made a dumb mistake, admit it. Now learn from it. Ask yourself why you did it. Keep that close, so in the future you can do better, strive for better. In the present, all you can do is aim to do better next time. Above all else, move on. Don't hide your past inside, and don't try to erase it from your history. Know what you did and try not to make the same mistake next time. Don't forget, or not care, but don't let it control you. You are more than your past mistakes.

Rather than be regretful, maybe we should be thankful for every mistake. Think about the technique of "trial and error" in science, also called a "heuristic method of problem solving, repair, tuning, or obtaining knowledge." Basically, you try and if it's a mistake, learn from it and try something else – then repeat until you find success.

Regret scares us. We blame ourselves. We think too much, and we hate ourselves. Let it go. This isn't a Disney movie, but let it go. Learn, and go make more mistakes until you find your success.

REPLACED

*I just believe that you have to allow each
other to grow in the way you're meant to
grow and not be afraid of losing that person,
because if you grow apart, then you grow
apart, and that's the way it was meant to be.*
— Jean-Philip Grobler

We replace things all the time when they're broken. So, too often when we're replaced, we feel as if we are the problem, as if we are broken. You may feel replaced by one person or a group of people. It is easy to feel replaced, broken, like no one wants you.

You may lose a friendship, but you are not replaced - you are unique and irreplaceable. You are also not broken in any way. Some things don't work out, for many reasons, and it doesn't mean the reason is you. When you are left alone, you will be found by other people. You change and grow, and life does go on. In the long run, you will gain and lose friends. This is normal even though every time you may feel you are losing a friend; it can be hard to accept.

Things come and go, and it's easy to feel as if people just pass you by. Sometimes, people don't actually replace you. It may feel like it, but if you are wondering, just ask. Sometimes all it takes is an honest conversation, so try to say how you feel.

Sometimes by feeling replaced, we draw away from people and can make it come true by our own actions – don't let that happen to you. If you care about someone, reach out, even if you worry they are pulling back from you. Then you will know the truth, and that's better than holding back and questioning everything. An honest discussion could provide the clarity you need.

Some people, unfortunately, will pass you by, and it may hurt. Being replaced says more about the person who left than the one left behind. If someone replaces you, it doesn't mean you're broken; they may have left for some dumb reason, or because of their own issues.

Even if someone replaces you because of who you are, they aren't someone you need in your life. But it is more likely that you may have naturally grown apart, each following your own path. Being replaced happens. We replace items all the time, and in relationships we might think that we are that old, useless part when someone replaces us. But people are different than refrigerators and dishwashers.

When someone leaves you or replaces you, they lose too. They don't get to enjoy and appreciate all your amazing qualities - it may feel like you have none and that's why they left, but that isn't true. It's so easy to blame yourself in times like this, but resist that temptation. You are perfectly you, and you deserve better.

Try to cherish what you shared, rather than mourn what was lost. It may seem like life won't be the same, but out there is someone new waiting for the blessing that will be your friendship. They will love and appreciate you and share new experiences with you.

SAD

like to think of "sad" as an umbrella that can pretty much be paired with, or is a less specific form of, all other negative emotions. The umbrella is what protects everything above and below it. Without knowing what it is to feel dry, we would not feel wet. If we never felt sad, we wouldn't know what it means to be happy. Emotions are complicated – not even science can begin to understand them fully. Being sad is never fun, but is a necessary part of life. Sadness can follow any unfortunate event or circumstance. Sometimes we even feel sad for simply no reason – it's just one of those days (normally Mondays!).

If you are sad, there is no reason to hide it or be ashamed. We all get sad. We recognize true art by its ability to connect to us and provoke an emotional response. I cry at movies where the dog dies. This is a mild sadness, but sadness nonetheless.

Sadness almost feels weak compared to other emotions in this book, but it's not. It is one of the strongest though. Sadness is hard to describe, except by saying it is the opposite of happiness. Look at every single emotion in this book – almost all of them relate to sadness in some way. We feel sad for a million reasons. It's a frequent part of human experience. So, don't feel like you need to hide your sadness – express it.

We all need help sometimes, so you should practice asking for help. Talk to someone. Get a friend who will cry with you when you need them, but also lift you up. Express your feelings. If you try bottling it up, it will either eventually all come out or it will always haunt the back of your mind.

Emotions can challenge us. We must not let them control who we are, but they are messages we send to ourselves, so we should pay attention to them. Experiencing sadness is normal. Don't let it hang around, though. Do what you can to seek happiness. Take out your sadness in a healthy way. Go work out, or write, or make art. We all have certain things that relieve ourselves, and we can use these things to nudge our state of mind to a better place.

Sadness. The base negative feeling. The feeling from which stems so many other bad feelings. An important emotion, but one we must overcome. We can overcome. Sadness is so broad it's hard for me to say anything that might address your situation. My advice is don't trust your gut, trust your heart. Think about what you can do to overcome this negative feeling, and don't let sadness linger.

I also believe that you can increase happiness by practicing gratitude and serving others. Be thankful for the blessings in your life and be a blessing to others in your life – these are true ways to increase joy and decrease sadness in yourself and others.

Overcome and create happiness. Spread happiness. Breathe happiness. Be happy.

SCARED

Life is too short to be scared and not take
risks. I'd rather be the person that's like, 'I
messed up,' than, 'I wish I did that.'
—Justine Skye

Being scared can be caused by fear, and pure fear is being afraid. The two are very similar, yet being scared is more of an action – being in a state of fear or nervousness – while being afraid means *feeling* fear or unease.

Being scared is something your friends might point out, that might give you goosebumps, or might prevent you from doing something. When you feel scared, first ask yourself: are you scared of doing something or are you scared of the possible outcome? Often it can be both, but usually we are more scared of what will happen as an effect of what we do.

Being scared can stop us from doing something. Perhaps in ancient times, this feeling developed as an indicator for a what to do or not to do. Still, today we may use this feeling to help us make a decision. In that sense, some fear is good, but it isn't good when it limits our ability to experience life.

We may be scared of potential negative outcomes like failing, but when we don't do something because we are scared, we definitely miss both the experience and the possible positive outcomes. Life isn't just about results. I know it may seem like they determine your life, but *you* determine your life.

If you're scared to do something against the rules, then you might want to listen to that message. There is always a reward-versus-risk factor and it's okay to feel scared sometimes. Being scared is one way of recognizing a risk we want to avoid. Think about the experience and whether the reward is worth the risk. I encourage you to really think about it and make a thoughtful choice, rather than letting your fear make the choice.

Life can scary, and when you don't know what to do, it is even scarier. The number of people out there who are scared of the amazing things they could be doing is insane. If we all rose up above the things we are most scared of, think of what we could do! Sure, some things might go wrong, but we would also learn along the way. Take risks, smart risks, the right risks, but risks, nonetheless. If you are scared of doing something, sometimes you have to just say, "whatever," and go with it.

When you do this, you will sometimes fall. You will mess up, and you will sometimes feel regret, but like I said before, there is the experience and outcome and maybe even growth and learning. Maybe you spend a couple of hours working towards a backflip on a trampoline, and then when you finally attempt it, you break your wrist. Well, that is a terrible accident, but wasn't the two hours of working up to the flip fun?

Things like this will happen, and sometimes your fears will come true – all I can say is live life. Make the best decisions you can, but when being scared controls who you are, you aren't you.

SELF-CONSCIOUS

*Teenage years are hard. And, having taught
high school for a number of years, I think
they're particularly hard on teenage girls. The
most self-conscious human beings on the
planet are teenage girls.*
—Rob Thomas, Matchbox Twenty

One thing, in all my teenage years, I've failed to understand is one's self-view. We see beauty all around us, all the time. So many positive people can point out every good thing about someone or something, and yet they fail to see the perfection within. Their perspective on themselves is often damaged by others. Their self-view is spoiled by the comparison of themselves to others.

Self-consciousness can even be fueled by jealousy and the bitterness that follows. Whatever may cause self-consciousness, we often have a negative or terrible opinion of ourselves. We are quick to notice the bad and we can't even affirm the good. Why this tendency is so common in teenage years is a question that we don't need an answer to, but rather a solution.

Some people won't shy away from pointing out your flaws and every single little thing you do wrong. They won't skip the chance to make themselves look or feel better by making you feel worse. That sometimes isn't their direct intention, but deep down it may be a result of their own self-consciousness.

So, we are all self-conscious and thus tear each other down? Yes, in a sense, that's exactly what we are and do. All it takes to make a change is one person, and that person could be you. Or me, I want to be different in that way too.

Be confident, and rather than making others jealous, help them gain perspective. Pay it forward, even if you think you are the first one paying. What others say doesn't matter – it truly doesn't. Just because someone says something it doesn't mean it's true. Or even if it's true, it doesn't mean it is bad. For you are you – you have value, advantages and strengths and you should learn to recognize and love them even if others don't.

Embrace your gifts and your flaws. Love yourself, and admit your mistakes and weaknesses. Don't deny them, but accept them. When you do these things, the opinions of others will not change your own. Your opinions of yourself should be cemented in a firm foundation of self-honesty.

Many of us we look at certain qualities – attractiveness, athleticism, success, popularity – that we see in other people and we sit, stare, and think. Our thoughts can lead us down a path of negativity and envy. We see the prettiest person in the world and instead of being proud of them, we are jealous. Jealousy brings bitterness and disappointment – in this sense, disappointment of ourselves.

You may think you can't be the prettiest in the world, but you already are. Beauty is in the eye of the beholder. Stop comparing yourself to people who are "better looking" or rich or famous and feeling sorry for yourself. Don't hate yourself because you're not like them. The only one deciding you are not that is you. Embrace who you are, because being you is the single greatest gift you can give.

If you start to recognize your own strengths and blessing, it can help curb the effect of comparison. To really stop it in its tracks, you must consciously try to stop the action itself. Human nature is to compare each other, especially to anyone who is better or worse than you at anything. If we think we are better, that can sometimes make us feel good about ourselves, but in the long run, I think we can be happier and healthier if we measure ourselves against our own best potential and not against others.

We must build up our confidence inside. A firewall, one built with self-love and self-appreciation. We spend so much money every year on security for everything in our lives, but we fail to value and guard ourselves. Wouldn't you leap to the defense of a friend and extoll their virtues? Then, in your mind, leap to your own defense as well.

You are fantastic just the way you are, so stop believing you're not. Don't change for others, love yourself. Life is too short to not like the person you are, and I know you are special and have strengths to be proud of. Don't listen to others who want to put you down. Don't sabotage yourself, but have faith in yourself. Self-love and confidence will bring you emotionally to a place better than ever. All it takes is determination and confidence. In the good days, the bad days, and the ugly days, guard your heart above all else.

SINGLE

I honestly think being single's great.
Being in a relationship's great.
It's all about the timing.
—Mila Kunis

ingle simply means that you are not part of a pair or group – or not dating a special someone. But if you say, "I feel single," you probably mean that you are around people that have found a special someone and you want that too.

With age, our longing for connection and love grows. It's hard to look around and see others in love when we have not found it ourselves. The absence of love now, however, does not mean you will be single forever – it only means you are single right now.

If a lot of our friends are in a relationship, feeling single can be especially hard. Like a lot of emotions, it can start a negative self-dialogue in our minds. One where we worry nobody loves us because we are not good enough or pretty enough to be loved. We can begin to worry that nobody is ever going to love us, which could then lead to behavior that makes us harder to love. Yikes!

It is okay to be single, so don't judge yourself by whether you are part of a pair. You do not need to pursue love, but if love comes to you, don't let it change who you are. Be yourself, so the other person gets to know the real you, rather than pretending to be a person you think they'd like.

I can't guarantee success, or that your crush will love you back. Just know that you don't really choose who you like. If someone doesn't like you, that doesn't mean you don't measure up in some way – every single person is unique and amazing in their own way, but not always a good match. You are unique and just because you haven't found the right person who loves you for you doesn't mean it's never going to happen.

Understand that love is a two-way street. Go crazy, but don't <u>be</u> crazy. Put your love where you will receive love back, and then your love will grow. Being single isn't a downfall or a flaw. It is a waiting period, so practice your patience. Don't look for just anyone, look for someone that is great for you.

Being single is absolutely okay. Too many people rely on a relationship for their identity or their self-worth, thinking that if someone likes them, it validates that they are likeable. Really, though, absolutely anyone could fill that role and why would you want just anyone?

Seek friends and really get to know people. Equally important – get to know yourself! Know what you like, so that you'll be better able to recognize it when you meet a friend with potential for some sort of deeper connection, even if that deeper connection is not a boyfriend or girlfriend, but a lifelong best friend.

There is a time for everything, so keep your options open and work on becoming your best self in the meantime. Don't let lack of immediate success determine the amount of long-term success you can have, because there is a fish in that big sea looking for you, just like you're looking for them.

SOCIALLY ANXIOUS

You can't let someone else lower your self-esteem, because that's what it is - self-esteem. You need to first love yourself before you have anybody else love you.
—Winnie Harlow

Social anxiety is a specific form of anxiety, one that impacts so many. I haven't experienced this myself, but I've seen it in the eyes of others. In the teenage years, through teenage eyes, fitting in and having friends is a top priority. So, when it feels virtually impossible to have them, or hang out with others, it is scary. All you want is to have friends, but it's hard to do that when it feels like the whole world is against you.

Whenever you're in groups, the eyes seem to always be turned toward you. Every whisper, murmur, and look must mean someone is judging you or hating you. You have to fit in, you must fit in. Yet, it never feels like you do. Fear keeps you quiet and locks you inside.

I understand what it is like to feel hated. Being shy, it's normal to feel this way, but this is about more than being shy. It's something many live with every day. School, parties, and get-togethers all bring challenges. Here is the thing about people though: every single person is worried about being judged or looking good. So, when you are with people, remember that they are more worried about themselves and aren't so worried about you.

When someone does make a comment, it is usually out of insecurity or jealousy. They call you ugly because they feel they aren't as pretty. You can see how we all are a little messed up. I promise you, being judged isn't the worst thing in the world. Don't live your life in fear, because, in the end, human relationships breed happiness.

It can also be scary. Everybody has a fear of rejection or denial, especially if they have been rejected or denied before. Afraid of the embarrassment of people not liking you.

None of what I'm about to say may seem doable, but trust me, it is. I've seen the most socially anxious person I know make new friends in a snap. Where you are at, it may be easier for you to sit alone in your room, rather than go out, but I believe you can build great friendships if that's what you want.

For us teens, fitting in really is like a badge you work to get. Making friends, being social ... it can take work and can be exhausting if you are naturally an introvert who needs "alone time." About half of all people are extroverts who are naturally more social and thrive while interacting with other people. They think its "normal," but don't understand that being shy or needing alone time is normal too. So, don't judge yourself by their standard or any standard except what's right for you.

Nothing great is easy. Build yourself up, and talk to your close friends about your issues. True friends will not judge you; they will support you. Start easy and work your way up. Go into social situations with confidence and hope, with positive self-talk, rather than fear. You will find a place where you fit in, but not based on popularity. You will fit in when you have people you can talk to and who care for you. They might be right in front of you!

I know that sometimes it feels everybody is against you, even those close to you. You could probably live your life thinking like that and isolating yourself, but for what? You must put yourself out there and have faith. Don't be afraid of messing up or being rejected – we all will face these hardships.

You are going to make new friends and be the person you want to be. When you are socially anxious, take some steps to calm down, and put yourself out there. Slowly but surely, you will get there. Don't think of it as fitting in, but as finding your people. You will fit because you will find the people you fit with as you are.

Here are some words from a friend of mine who deals with social anxiety. Know you are never alone on this issue. Social Anxiety often requires help by a professional, so don't hesitate to seek allies and support. I have listed some resources at the end of this book that might be a start.

As I walk down the hallway at school, I see a group of girls. They start to laugh, and one looks at me and then looks back at her friends. Are they laughing at me? Does it have to do with the way I'm dressed? Or is it my hair?

I walk to the bathroom to look in the mirror. Nothing is wrong. I like the way my outfit looks, and I like the way my hair is today. Then why are they laughing at me?

They're not. They're laughing at some stupid Instagram post, and I just freaked out for nothing. Then I remember those girls are my friends, and it turns out I just completely overthought everything.

I get socially anxious a lot, and to be honest, it is not the best feeling; it causes me to spend hours worrying about my appearance. Social anxiety also causes me to stop being who I am in front of people who should accept me and who have already told me they accept me for who I am.

Social anxiety is hard to overcome. It's even hard to admit you have it, but in the end, you are who you are, and nobody should change that. You were made to be special and you were made to be who you are, so why try to change it? Just so you can "fit in"? That is the thing: fitting in is just all in your mind. Stay true to who you are--you were made to stand out.

STRESSED

You must learn to let go. Release the stress.
You were never in control anyway.
—Steve Maraboli

The emotion that can grow and get worse as you get older and life gets more complicated. Added responsibilities, waiting to the last minute, upcoming tests or assessments that could decide your future ... whatever it is, we all feel stressed. But we all can make it through, and we can even sometimes use stress to our advantage.

Many of us feel like everything in life is building up, and we have very little time to finish all the things that need to be done. In the moment, it feels like every incomplete task is going to be the end of the world. Stress is an emotion that builds tension within, and tests your patience and virtue. Stress may even be caused by one thing, blown out of proportion, making us believe it will change our whole lives. The reality is, some things may change your life, and it could even end up being an improvement.

One good thing to do when you feel stressed is find your calming mechanism. This could be something like a breathing exercise or something small, like petting your dog. Maybe you just need a little alone time or maybe you need to spend some time surrounded by friends. Maybe escaping into a good book helps you get back to a good place. We all have different things that calm us, and it's important to identify and use these strategies to step back from whatever is stressing us to clear our minds. Once we reduce stress in the situation, we can really consider what's going on.

Let's say you have three homework assignments due tomorrow – and you're stressed about finishing it all. First, take a breath and plan out how you will do them. Plan the work and work the plan, as they say! Have a test too? You can study. You may have already done so and are still freaking out. If that's the case, think motivating thoughts. You will do the best you can do, and that's truly all you can do.

Whatever situation or task is causing you stress, it's helpful to calm down and think rationally – but not overthink and let your mind spiral down a negative street. Keeping calm and coming up with a strategy can help you reduce the level of stress, so then you can do each thing one step at a time.

In life, we will all get stressed, so accept it and prepare for it. Try to figure out your preferences and healthy coping mechanisms and use them to manage your stress. Don't let stress force you into negative reactions – control your actions. Self-discipline can be helpful, and you can work on improving yours. Developing even a little control over your situation could help reduce your stress, so whatever is stressing you out, go out there and work on fixing it. You can and will do great things!

STUCK

You're stuck with being yourself, so the
important thing is to find people who like
that.
—*Andrew Davies*

I write this to share with you. This is the first thing I ever wrote to try and help a friend, and this small section would lead me to writing the rest of the chapters. The idea of a book was not even an idea. I left it unchanged, and it is exactly the same as it was in the Note section on my phone.

Sometimes we feel stuck; this is due to problems and complications. There are two types of problems in this world. 99.9 percent of problems can be divided into one of these categories: problems that can be solved and problems that can't be solved.

If a problem can be solved or has a reachable solution, it is a temporary problem. You can overcome this problem, whatever it is. Plan how you will do it. Then take actions, step-by-step, until you have ultimately solved a problem.

If a problem does not have a reachable solution, or it is controlled by outside factors, it is a problem of the mind. It would be like me, alone, trying to take on global warming. Just wouldn't work. So, I cannot spend all day or stay up late at night worrying about global warming because it is not solvable in the state I am in. So, I must focus on myself and react to the problem. Stay patient and control and care about what you can control.

Either way, problems – big or small, solvable or unsolvable – are annoying, and you should spend a great deal of time thinking about them and talking them out with a person of trust and intellect.

STUPID

Everybody is a genius. But if you judge a fish
by its ability to climb a tree, it will live its
whole life believing that it is stupid.
—Albert Einstein

M odern society cares a lot about the youth, though from a youth perspective it can feel like pressure. One of the main pressures we experience is academics. A letter that labels how intelligent we might be. An online test that decides which math class we will be in for the next part of our lives. Tens of assignments, hundreds of questions, thousands of seconds in a week spent on school.

For some, we feel like we're not quite there. Math, language arts, social studies, or science may not be your strengths. You try hard and perhaps fall short. Your best is never good enough. These thoughts are easy to conceive, but for what? Your best is you, and life is more than core school subjects.

What is amazing to me is how every human seems to be good at different things. What's also amazing is how the system singles out a small percentage of these skills and focuses on them. Forces you to focus, study, remember and eventually master these skills. Which may be completely different than the set of skills you have.

I'm not saying quit school, by any means. I am saying you should never feel stupid because of school. Everyone is smart and gifted in their own way. So, don't spend your whole life trying to be an amazing mathematician if you're born to be an artist. The way things are, you must try your best in school, work hard, and get a tutor if necessary, because it could affect your future. So, every day try your best, and strive for the best you can do, but if your best isn't perfect, that's okay.

Even if you haven't discovered it yet, I firmly believe there is something that you are gifted in. It could be problem-solving, math, art, music, computers, building people up, leadership, positivity, writing, reading, cooking, crafts, working with animals, understanding nature, exploration, swimming, sports, YouTube, life hacks, public speaking, creativity, or one of endless other skills and talents. No matter what it is, your gift is amazing – it's unique; it's you.

Embrace your gifts, no matter what. You may be good at the weirdest thing ever, but you're good at it for a reason. Don't let the fact that your strengths don't align with modern standards and expectations ever make you feel less important than you are.

When we lose all those gifts, skills, and opportunities, we lose the very thing that allowed the human race to be such a diverse species. We must stop generalizing talents and learn to accept all. I'm asking you to start by accepting and embracing your very own gifts. No two brains are the same, and that individuality should be celebrated. There's a difference between being smart and getting high test scores, so find it. No letter or number will ever determine how "smart" you are.

TRAPPED

*As a teenager, I felt so hemmed in and
trapped, both by the place I lived and the
expectations others had about school, college,
and a future career.* —Sabaa Tahir

Life presents situations that we don't know how to solve. Situations where we aren't sure what to do, so we end up doing nothing. We do nothing from fear of doing the wrong something, and we feel trapped. Here is the thing: much of life is going to be new and situational. Every situation is going to be different, and I can't give you the key and tell you which door to go through, but I can try my best to help you create doors to walk through.

So, you're stuck, and you don't know what to do. That's reasonable. As you grow, things get progressively harder and always newer, but you also gain more control. We can't be expected to always know what to do, but people are counting on us to do the right thing, or we are counting on ourselves to do the right thing. Any step is better than no step, but it's best to find the right step. The problem is you do not know the right step. The truth is, every step can be the right step if you try your best. You can learn from any step you take – and that was the point after all – so take a step.

If you feel trapped, seek a way out. Find several ways out. They are there, just learn to recognize them. Whether in your mind, or aloud, discuss which one is best, and go with it. Advocate for yourself to escape. There are ways out, and any way out is a step in the right direction if you think it is. Do your best to escape the situation, and that's all you can do. Don't sit there and pout and expect the problem to solve itself. Actively solve the problem. You know the problem better than I do, so take risks, but be smart. Do something that you can look back on and smile.

It may seem as if I'm just saying that there are simple solutions to the problems you face, and there may not be. Simple or not, it is possible if you make it possible. I have faith in every single person to find a way out. You can find a way out of your problem, and you will, if you are persistent. Far too often this is the biggest obstacle in our trap – taking the first step.

For some of you, you may feel trapped in a more serious situation involving physical or mental abuse and may feel helpless. Your first step may be to ask help of a trusted adult or counselor. Or, your step may just be doing your best, learning and preparing for the day when you are old enough to leave and make your own way as an adult. I may never meet you, but I want to encourage you.

UGLY

You should take some responsibility for the way you present yourself. But you should not be hung up on your looks, whether you are ugly or handsome, because it isn't an achievement.
—Christopher Reeve

Self-image is often influenced by the dumbest things, in my opinion. Some of us don't feel comfortable leaving the house without makeup on. Let that sink in. Some of us feel we need a product just to live up to society's "standards." Let me start by telling you that you are not ugly. It doesn't surprise me that someone would think that in our modern world though.

We see images that are edited, manipulated, "face tuned," and think we need to look like that. We see the best-looking people at our school and think we need to try to be as attractive as them. So, people will like us, so people will think good things about us. We do all this to impress and please others.

Beauty is a weird thing. We were not put on this planet to go through life looking nice and trying to impress others. You are not ugly, and every single person is unique and beautiful, but when we start to compare ourselves to others, it's no wonder we think we are anything but beautiful.

We should all hope to reach a point in life where you see that looks don't matter. Your love life will come from someone who thinks you are the most attractive person in the world, even if you think you're not. Good people won't think worse of you or not like you because of your physical appearance. The people you need in your life won't be affected by your looks.

You should also try to be happy with your looks. Beauty is in the eye of the beholder. You are who you are, and that's what makes you beautiful. Isn't it so wonderful that every person is different, and no two look the same? That's truly amazing! Just because you don't look like a "model" doesn't mean you are any less pretty. You don't need makeup; you don't need to spend anything on a product to "fix" the way you look. Wear what you want to wear if it makes you happy. Don't spend your whole life trying to impress others. With the way style changes, that will be a never ending battle and will never make you happy anyway. Do it for yourself, and realize your beauty.

You are not ugly. Everyone looks a certain way, but that shouldn't influence us in any way. Be confident in your own body, because it's yours. Don't try to impress anyone but yourself. Be you – you are perfect just the way you are. The number one thing to remember, about yourself and others, is that true beauty is on the inside.

UNCONFIDENT

Optimism is the faith that leads to
achievement. Nothing can be done without
hope and confidence.
—Helen Keller

We look to other people in life so much. We hear the opinions of others, and we so often listen. We see people "better" than us, and we start to see ourselves as worse than we are. We feel in our hearts that we are not good enough. Because of this, we lose confidence. We let outside factors ruin our confidence, and it is truly sad, because that is what others sometimes set out to do.

Makeup companies make advertisements with edited images of models, and you feel so bad about yourself and think you need makeup to look pretty. You don't. Lack of confidence costs you.

At some point in our lives, me decide who we care about and who we don't. From there, we decide whose opinion we care about – and it truly should only be your own and those we love and trust. We are the ones that decide our lives. But how do we not care about the opinions of others? The only way to do this is to have self-assurance for everything you do – have confidence.

You don't need to be perfect to be confident, you just need to know yourself and have faith in yourself. That's true for everyone – even that airbrushed model on the cover of a magazine. You are who you are, and you were made to be this way. Start to see the potential in yourself. Realize that you are not perfect, and that's why you are perfect – perfectly you. Confidence is a foundation upon which every brick in the building may remain sturdy.

For me, being confident is not an achievement, but takes ongoing work. Learning more about myself, both strengths and weaknesses, helps me understand the things I can do myself and when I might need to ask for help. In that sense, it can be hard work to be confident. It may seem like a weird concept until you think of confidence as something you build. Sometimes others try to tear it down and then I have to work to build it back up for myself again.

We may not currently be self-motivated, and let me tell you why. When you are confident, it is like the engine in your car. It lives on the inside, but it allows the car to run and get places. Your confidence will shield you from the opinions of people with no importance in your life. It will guide you to the right places. It will help you do things to change the world, things you never thought you could do. You may not get anything you want, but you will get a shot – take your shot. You will pursue happiness, and you will get there, even if it looks different than you previously imagined. All because of a little faith, a little motivation, a little self-respect, a little self-knowledge ... and some work.

So many of us lack confidence because we are afraid. Fear stops us, but confidence shields us.

Make changes, be yourself, strive for better, strive for the best. We all have areas where we can improve and working on them can help too. This may be contradicting, but we should all asses what we aren't so good at, what we do that has negative impacts on ourselves and others, and try to improve these things. When you do, each success will help you build confidence.

Whatever the reason you aren't confident – a person, a past experience – you can get past it. Your future, your potential, and the possibilities you have are without limit. Go through life confidently, because you are the best person for you. You are best position to change your own life, and you can do it. And you will do it confidently. Don't let any other person determine how you feel about yourself.

UNIMPORTANT

No matter how small and unimportant what
we are doing may seem, if we do it well, it
may soon become the step that will lead us to
better things. —Channing Pollock

This emotion really brings together a lot of other feelings discussed in this book. Feeling unimportant isn't a one-time, five-minute thing--it isn't even a phase. It's something we feel about ourselves, and we don't even think about it--until we do.

When we feel unimportant, we often compare. We can lose confidence and we begin to create false views of who we are. Worst of all, we may begin to accept this viewpoint. When you think you are not important you think you don't deserve as much as others. This emotion can reach a point where you feel so unimportant that you think you deserve the pain. You feel unimportant to everybody, so you feel unimportant in the world. It's not easy, but you have to talk out of this. Live and breathe reasons to be important.

Feeling unimportant is just a feeling and a judgement we are making about ourselves – it's not who you really are. You are important. Every day you may wake up and compare yourself to the best person at everything. You may let a letter decide how smart you are. You may allow likes to determine how pretty or popular you are. You may let one person's opinion ruin your day, your week, or after enough time, your life. Soon enough, you let all the little things in life erode your happiness and your potential. You may decide you are not important and because you do, you limit yourself. Don't let others measure your importance and don't accept their labels.

I have no idea where you come from, what your past is like, what you've done, or what's been done to you. I may never know. I don't need to. The fact that you were put on Earth was a 1 in 400,000,000,000,000,000 chance. The fact that you are alive and reading this today is enough. The fact that you made it this far in life is enough.

It doesn't matter what you have done or what others think of you. We all mess up. We all have good and bad days. These days do not determine how valuable we are. You're priceless – this world needs you. You may be going through the motions and feel as if you have nothing going for you. Soon enough, the luck will roll your way. You will find an opportunity and you will take it.

Life is a gift. Don't go through it thinking you don't deserve to live out this gift. You are here for a reason, and if you let other people tear you down, they will literally strip you of the reason you were put here. We too often change how we think because of the influence of others.

You have to believe in your importance - appreciate yourself, love yourself. You are unique and different - this is a blessing! Discover your gifts and use them. When you do, other may try to tear you down because of their own limitations. Even so, all you can do is smile, inside and out because you know your worth.

Focus on yourself. In the end, only you will be the reason your life was or was not amazing. You are important. I believe it, and I can say it, but it doesn't mean anything if you don't believe it too.

UNLIKED

*We think sometimes that poverty is only being
hungry, naked and homeless. The poverty of
being unwanted, unloved and uncared for is
the greatest poverty. We must start in our own
homes to remedy this kind of poverty.*
—Mother Teresa

It's easy to feel as if no one likes you. In fact, in the teenage years, through school, that is probably a common feeling for so many. All it takes is one time when people didn't like you, one time they didn't want to hang out or talk with you, and you start to feel unliked. Multiple times, you feel unwanted, even if it wasn't the case, and you start to believe it.

Many people won't like you along the way, but those people don't matter at all. If they don't like you, they don't deserve you. You should care about and find the people who do care about you and like you for you. Those kinds of people will make the ones who don't like you dissipate from memory.

Many people will unlike or dislike you, people can be mean like that. When they do, it doesn't mean you are a bad person or that there is something wrong with you. You are great, and a few opinions don't determine what kind of person you are. You determine what kind of person you are.

Don't try to be someone else to fit in. Be yourself, be good, be you. Learn to like yourself before seeking acceptance from others. How can you expect others to appreciate you if you don't appreciate yourself? Don't try too hard to make someone like you, don't change to fit in, don't do stuff you wouldn't normally – be yourself.

This can be hard to do and hard to accept. We often forget that not everyone is going to like us. Even if most people won't get you, if only 1 percent of people are your kind of people, that means you have 77 million people as potential future friends. So, go out there and find them!

Go find people who might have similar interests and connect with them. Put yourself out there, and don't let anything stop you. If you fail to connect with someone and you want to be liked, don't get discouraged. They are not always going to run into you, but if you keep looking, you will find someone who accepts you and with whom you can connect.

Don't ever put it on yourself if you feel unliked. You should be yourself, and find people who you connect with, and that will bring you happiness. Along the way, remember something my mom tells me: to have a friend, you have to be a friend.

UNMOTIVATED

Although circumstances may change in the
blink of an eye, people change at a slower
pace. Even motivated people who welcome
change often encounter stumbling blocks that
make transformation more complicated than
they'd originally anticipated.
—Amy Morin

'm writing this exactly one year after I broke my hip. A weird bone to break, and it led me to a period where I was on crutches and unmotivated to do a lot of things. There's no doubt that life knocks us down, and sometimes we need a reason to get back up and can't find one.

In time, you will see the reason doesn't come from anybody else, but from that place where Americans put our right hand during the Pledge of Allegiance. It comes from our heart. It comes from loving ourselves and having faith in the future. We all feel unmotivated at times. Some of us can't get out of bed on Monday morning without our alarm clocks. Others don't see why they should keep pushing themselves – in school, in life, in a relationship – when there is no progress. It's tough to work hard for what feels like nothing.

This emotion creates an awkward stage of nothingness – no good, but no bad. A very awkward pause. So, what you have to do to solve this awkwardness is take a first step, which isn't easy for many. Just go out there and attack it. Attack your day, and attack your laziness. Those chains holding you back are nothing compared to your potential. There is only one thing worse than being unmotivated, which is the realization, after an awkward period of time, that we got nothing done. We must fight every second against this.

Some days, truthfully, I didn't want to write the chapters in this book. When that happened, I made myself a deal to just write one page and then I could stop. That first step sometimes led to more steps. When I feel unmotivated, I think of the ones I love. While I don't always want to do it for myself, I'm sometimes willing to do it for others. I use that.

Recognizing your feeling of being unmotivated is really a good thing, because now you know you need to do something to break out of it. I believe you can get better at this with practice. Take a first step. Pick a task and do it, even though you don't want to – maybe hang up your clothes or clean off your dresser. Make yourself go for a ten minute walk around the block. I find that sometimes, if I do something active, even a quick walk, it can change my outlook completely for the rest of the day.

UNWANTED

It hurts the most when the person that made
you feel special yesterday makes you feel so
unwanted today.
—Rashida Rowe

You know what's unwanted: things that don't provide any value, purpose, or use. In this world, we can sometime feel like we have no value, no purpose, or no use. And then we feel like an old, junky object – unwanted. You've probably heard the saying, "one man's trash is another man's treasure." You may feel like you are trash to someone, and if they make you feel that way, dissolve the bonds of your friendship. You are wanted by someone, and neither of you may even know it yet.

It may seem like the world and its people don't want you. They may not see your worth, and sometimes you may not even see your own worth. If that's you, you first have to provide confidence in yourself. You are not an old stereo – and even if you are, lots of people love stereos!

Don't define your success by whether the cool people want you. You naturally come with talents, and that uniqueness is great. Don't change yourself, for those are the gifts that make you special. You don't buy a microwave to freeze your beans. Everything is unique and wanted in its own special way.

You may feel like a defected product, but you're not – you are a person. Every person will find other people. People who want them, who will appreciate them. You will be found, in time. Make it easier on yourself, because you don't always meet people just by chance.

Put yourself out there, and when you do, be yourself. Be who you are, and when you come across people who don't treat you right, move on from them. Go out there and meet new people, show them who you are. As badly as you want to be wanted, someone else wants to be too.

Try to have patience and don't give up. You are a human, and we are relational creatures. By embracing yourself and your gifts, by confidently being who you are, you will make it easier for your people to find you. So, don't wear a mask to try to be something different for others. Be open to the people who see you for who you are and discover what you have in common. These people will make you feel appreciated and satisfy your needs. And don't forget to give that back to others as well – we all just want someone who wants us.

WEAK

You gain strength, courage, and confidence by every experience in which you really stop to look fear in the face. You are able to say to yourself, 'I lived through this horror. I can take the next thing that comes along.'
—Eleanor Roosevelt

Strength can be described as what gets us through the obstacles we encounter in life. Strength is also the quality that allows us to pick something up. Physically, it might be a heavy barbell. Emotionally speaking, it is the ability to pick ourselves up through hardship. So, naturally, when weakness comes upon us it's hard to carry on.

The harder your past has been, the stronger you will be. A recent past filled with pain may make us temporarily weak, and when we feel weak it brings an array of feelings that make even everyday tasks difficult. Just like any soreness, bruise, bump, or scratch, it will heal stronger than it was before. Protect yourself by carrying on, letting less things affect you, and avoiding things you know are bad for you. You wouldn't want to rub dirt on a scratch, so avoid this by moving on.

Life can take a toll on us. It can knock us down and weaken us. The best thing to do is simple – get back up. People will tear you down, emotionally. It will get to you, and the continuation of pain can add up and make you weak. You may feel as if you can't go on, as if you need to give up.

Have you ever wondered where strength comes from? It comes from the inside and it is something you can build up over time. Just like you might build up your muscles by lifting weights, each time you face an emotional or mental challenge, you can build up your inner strength.

You will have ups and downs. You will feel weak sometimes. If you're reading this, you may be having a tough time right now. You might be mentally exhausted, even if your body isn't tired. Don't feel bad about needing a mental break, take it and rest yourself. But also use the time to plan for how you will keep going.

Find someone or something to work for, and let that inspire you. Work hard, but also work smart. You don't need anyone to push you; the thought of feeling better is going to push you. The light at the end of the tunnel is never reached if we give up halfway through the tunnel.

Life will knock you down, and those who can get back up and fight are the ones who will build their strength and be successful. My best days are often the ones where I don't feel like doing anything. For some reason, I have a hard time getting the ball rolling, as in getting things started, but if I push through and get the ball rolling, I can usually accomplish more than I imagined. I had a day like that recently when we had to run a mile at school. I felt like it was an off day, but I decided I would do my best anyway and I get a time to be proud of. Not my best time ever, but certainly not my worst!

Things get tough, and you will go through time when you just want to give up. Sometimes it is good to pause, but then to eventually get going again. Don't let emotions control you or limit you. The evil in the world draws its power from those who let the evil itself affect them. Rise above and be better. The strength is already in your heart; you just need to build on it.

WORRIED

*When you begin to worry, go find something
to do. Get busy being a blessing to someone;
do something fruitful. Talking about your
problem or sitting alone, thinking about it,
does no good; it serves only to make you
miserable. Above all else, remember that
worrying is totally useless. Worrying will not
solve your problem.*
—Joyce Meyer

Worried is a more mild form of anxious and stressed, but it's more common as well. This emotion sticks around and influences many other emotions. When you worry, you are scared to see the outcome of something that is yet to happen – or likely may not happen at all.

It's human nature to be scared, frightened, or even terrified of the unknown. Worry is this feeling. Maybe we have messed up, and now we are worried about what is going to happen because of our actions. We worry that maybe we aren't good enough for a person, or ready for a test. We're scared we will disappoint others or ourselves.

Unknown outcomes are scary – they cause a tremendous amount of feelings. You have to be prepared for whatever can happen, but above all else, I encourage you to be positive. Through positivity, you stand up to that fear, pushing it away. You do not know the outcome, and there are so many factors you can't control in the world. It's possible your feared outcome will come true, but if the outcome is out of your control, there's nothing you can do about that. Don't fear even if things go another direction than the one in which you were thinking, they can still result in a positive outcome. All you can control is you. Do your best. Hope for the best, prepare for the worst. If you do get an undesired outcome, it is an opportunity to learn and grow.

In the moments leading up to the activity or event that is making you nervous, try to do things that keep your mind off it. Take deep breaths, and think happy thoughts. When it's time, go out there and carry through with whatever is making you worried. In the end, no matter the outcome, you can learn and benefit from it in the long-term.

HAPPY

Your success and happiness lies in you.
Resolve to keep happy, and your joy and you
shall form an invincible host against
difficulties.
—Helen Keller

Be happy with being you. Love your flaws.
Own your quirks. And know that you are just
as perfect as anyone else, exactly as you are.
—Ariana Grande

This emotion wasn't requested by anyone, and it different than the rest of this book. But how can one encourage the spread of happiness without talking about? We all know what it is like to be happy. Even if you simply feel content, it's a stretch, but I would still call it happiness. We experience peak happiness, joy, usually after a big event, but sometimes just because it is a wonderful day.

For many, happiness always seems to be a stretch. For some, it is the norm. Either way, this chapter focuses on appreciating and spreading happiness. In this way, we create a more positive environment everywhere we go. The pursuit of happiness is important, and it's a pursuit we should all be in together.

We all have felt happiness. Most of us came into this world crying, but I like to believe happiness is the first real emotion we feel. What makes us happy changes with time. We should all aim for what makes up happy, whether it is achievable or not. Everything was once unachievable until someone achieved it. But hopefully you're reading this because you are happy, and now you need to know what to do next.

Maybe curiosity brought you to this chapter ... either way, I hope you will help me in encouraging others. If you are feeling good, confident, empowered, excited, proud, or happy – congratulations! I'm thankful for that and thankful for you.

We all also know what it is like to *not* feel happy. We know how quickly things can go sour. So, while you are happy, embrace it! Be yourself, and have fun, but above all else, try to spread that happiness by helping others.

Happiness is special, and through connections and real talk with other people, it's one very good way of changing someone's day from sour to sweet. You're happy – go you! Now help those who you love. Get out there and be risky ... step out of your comfort zone and take your shot.

This world probably has a hundred negative things coming just around the corner. Don't focus on those. instead, treasure this moment of happiness. Bring your friends and loved ones along for the ride.

It's important to be real too. Don't be fake-happy or phony. Express your feelings so they don't linger and fester inside. When the positive times come, enjoy them. Let them fill you, pay it forward and let the good outweigh the bad. For every bad thing in this world there are ten good things, and you, personally, are one of them. Whatever made you happy, be thankful. Never forget where you came from.

There is a reason this chapter is last – because it's different. Just like you, it's there when you need it.

GOODBYE

*Goodbyes are really just starting a new part of
your life and ending another. You need to
truly understand what you are saying
goodbye to before you leave. This might be
hard but the more you understand and accept
it, the easier it will get.*
—A Friend

I hope that when you finish this book you can say goodbye, not to me, but to your old self. Never forget where you came from, but strive to improve. Understand where you can be better and say goodbye to those parts of you. Step through a portal and change your life for the better. Start a new part of your life filled with happiness.

I wish you luck, but if you need a starting point with an emotion, I hope this book can help. May your days be filled with happiness. May the good days outshine the bad a hundred to one. May you be a beacon of hope and happiness for your friends and family. You will do great things. Do not let anyone in this world stop you. When a person rises up and jealousy steps in, the world will try to bring you back down. Don't let it. You change the world because you can.

From me, I give you my best.

MY ASK OF YOU

Whatever your race, financial status, age, gender, sexuality, home, past, body, I want to ask for your help. In his Nobel Prize acceptance speech, Holocaust survivor Elie Wiesel said, "What all these victims need above all is to know that they are not alone; that we are not forgetting them, that when their voices are stifled we shall lend them ours, that while their freedom depends on ours, the quality of our freedom depends on theirs."

Being on this planet, being alive, we have a call. A call to each other and to the world. This world may beat you down every day, and you may need help too. Emotionally, I hope you feel that you are not alone in this world while reading through these chapters, but as the human race, we can and must do more.

Think of any discrimination in this world, and how it is being solved. I'll tell you how: by someone speaking up. All it takes is one person, one person that gets other people on board. When you see something wrong in the world, big or small, do not stand silent. Do not sit there in fear. Do not let things slide by. You challenge it. Everything that happens ... you make sure it is for people. When people are silenced, lend them your voice. I don't care who you are. You have something that no one can take away, and that's your voice. When you see evil and wrong – will you speak? Will you confront it? I hope you will.

I get that standing up, being different, is hard. Yet, name anyone famous, or anyone we study in history who made a difference. Were they some ordinary person? Yes – until they decided to make a change. Sheep don't change the world. People who follow crowds, people who go through life just being bossed and herded around, don't aspire to much.

Those who were once a sheep, but now stand up to the wolves, are the heroes. Silence, in fact, is the biggest threat to every person. Advocate for yourself, advocate for others, advocate for good in the world. You have a voice, and it isn't limited to yourself. The world likes cookie – cutter people and for every person to learn and live the same way. In reality, no one is the same – promoting that truth is promoting diversity. The fact that no one is the same is what makes humanity special.

If you believe in sitting down all day, forty-hour work weeks, and doing something that gets you by, then go do it. If you believe in being different, sixty-hour work weeks, and doing something that makes this world better, that makes life better for all people, then go do it. There is nothing that can stop you. If you want something bad enough, go for it.

Everyone who changed the world took a stand. All those people were normal people who believed in something and ran with it. Don't accept excuses. I don't want this chapter to be something that merely inspires you, for inspiration sometimes only lasts a week. Let this be something that motivates real action.

So, to those who will change themselves, who will make this world a better place, I thank you. Think about this – at the end of your life, will you be proud of what you did? What will our legacy be to our children and our grandchildren? I hope that I live the rest of my life in a way that I will sit on my deathbed and smile, satisfied that I fought against the negative and added to the positive. I hope that for you too.

HOW TO FIND HELP

Mental health is a critical part of overall health. A range of great information is available to help you in any stage of distress at Mental Health America (MHA), www.mentalhealthamerica.net.

Serious mental health issues cannot be solved by a few words on a page, nor can they be solved alone.

If you or someone you know is experiencing serious emotional challenges, needs help or is in danger, please refer to this list of resources and reach out. Most are available 24 hours a day, 7 day a week.

Washington Resources

- **24-Hour Crisis Line:** 1 (866) 4CRISIS (427-4747) provides immediate help to individuals, families and friends of people in emotional crisis. www.crisisconnections.org
- **King County 2-1-1:** 2-1-1 or 1 (800) 621-4636 connects people to the help they need; comprehensive information on health and human services for King County, WA.
- **WA Recovery Help Line:** 1 (866) 789-1511 offers anonymous, confidential 24-hour help for Washington State residents experiencing substance abuse, gambling or mental health challenges. www.warecoveryhelpline.org
- **Teen Link Help Line:** 1 (866) TEENLINK (833-6546) offers a confidential, anonymous, and non-judgmental help line for youth ages 13-20, every evening between 6-10 p.m. 866teenlink.org
- **WA Warm Line:** 1 (877) 500-WARM (500-9276) is a peer support help line for people living with emotional and mental health challenges.
- **Joanna Dickenson, MSA:** 1 (619) 246-3937

National Resources

- **Teen Line:** 1 (310) 855-4673 (or text "TEEN" to 839863) a confidential hotline for teenagers which operates every evening from 6:00pm to 10:00pm PST. teenlineonline.org

- **Crisis Text Line:** Text HOME to 741741 from anywhere in the United States, anytime, about any type of crisis.
- **National Domestic Violence Hotline:** 1 (800) 799-SAFE (7233) trained advocates are available 24x7 to provide confidential support to anyone experiencing domestic violence or seeking resources and information.
- **TrevorLifeline:** 1-866-488-7386 (or **TrevorText** — text "START" to 678678) a safe and judgement-free 24x7 crisis intervention service for LGTBQ youth. www.thetrevorproject.org
- **National Suicide Prevention Lifeline:** (800) 273-TALK (8255) provides 24/7, free and confidential support for people in distress. suicidepreventionlifeline.org

You can also talk to a trusted friend or adult, like a school counselor. If you need any sort of help, for any sort of reason, get it. You have made it this far. You deserve happiness, so pursue it.

Maybe right now nothing seems to be working. You may be filled with pain and hatred and have been taking it out on yourself. Life may be bleak right now, but if you make it through this, there will be happiness down the road. It may seem out of reach, but trust me, it's there.

Everyone needs a helping hand now and then, so don't hesitate to ask for help. I love you, and you are worth it.

ABOUT THE AUTHOR

Parker Jones is a regular teenager from a little town about 30 miles east of Seattle, Washington. He hangs out with friends, plays soccer, has dog named May-Z (pronounced like Jay-Z) and likes online video games. (His parents sometimes complain he plays too much Fortnite.)

This is his first book. In addition to this book, Parker has also been teaching himself Swift-C and plans to release an app on the Apple app store later in the year. If you ask anyone, they'll tell you Parker is a great kid.

Still ... he sometimes struggles with negative emotions. And because of that, he wants other teens to know that, no matter what it looks like from across the room or on social media, everybody needs a helping hand sometime and that is absolutely okay.

You can find out more about what Parker is doing and connect with him at:

https://withparker.com

or email him at pjauthor@outlook.com

51867557R00096

Made in the USA
Lexington, KY
06 September 2019